Contents

1 What's it all about?

Here is a story about Nasrudin, *for centuries a central character in the legends of the East.*

A neighbour came to borrow Nasrudin's clothes line.

'I am sorry,' he said, 'but I am drying flour on it.'

'But how can you dry flour on a line?'

'It is less difficult than you think—when you don't want to lend it.'

This example demonstrates something about the workings of the human mind—the brain's capacity to rationalise. If we do not wish to accept or do something, we can always find 'good' reasons for not doing so—even to convincing ourselves it cannot be done. This story presents an accurate model of that process, even if nobody called it 'rationalisation' at the time.

Four basic questions

East is east and west is west ... and the twain are meeting as people seek alternative ways of knowing themselves.

There is no culture in the world that does not have its storehouse of psychological knowledge, its theories about the workings of the human mind. We have always searched for meanings and understanding, for answers to the basic questions—Who? What? How? Why? Our theories and beliefs have in the past often been couched in folklore, fables or mysticism—as they are today in societies less 'developed' than those of Europe and America. In westernised societies our approach to these questions has been along technological and statistical lines. We have started to develop a science of human behaviour, which we call psychology.

The fact that other cultures have not developed, or may not subscribe to, such an approach does not mean that their awareness of psychology or of human behaviour is less acute. On the contrary traditional 'stories', myths, can embody and are intended to convey subtle and complex psychological ideas, as the story of Nasrudin's clothes line demonstrates.

The cultures of the East have observed the workings of the mind and interpreted them in the 'everything-happening-together' form of the story. This is something that Western mainstream psychology did not fully come to terms with until the 1960s, when psychological information from the East became more readily accessible. But many years previously the Swiss psychologist Carl Gustav Jung, after breaking with the teachings

Psychologists use other means than scattered shells to reach their conclusions—but their aims still include the divination and prediction of why and how we do what we do.

5

Measuring, recording, observing—scientific psychology bases its findings on direct evidence of behaviour.

of Sigmund Freud, the father of psychoanalysis, had already begun to emphasise the importance of myth, and of Eastern philosophy, in understanding the life of the mind. And a school of psychology derived from the original psychoanalytic movement, the German *Gestalt* school, highlighted the 'wholeness' of human experience. But these were exceptions rather than the rule, which was to separate behaviour into approachable, isolated pieces for close inspection.

Now Western psychology tries to scrutinise information in a systematic way rather than to present it at the revealing but somewhat vague level of folklore, mysticism or symbolism requiring a high degree of intuition and wide familiarity with the history of particular cultures. It has tended to specialise in the experimental method derived from more traditional sciences, requiring of itself precise, logical, quantifiable, measured and controlled observation.

Contemporary psychology is undergoing the initial stirrings of the bringing together of these two types of approach. The 'everything-happening-together' or holistic approach to understanding, characteristic of the East—and sought after as the informing principle of 'personality' and 'social' psychology—is beginning once again to balance our scientific approach in a more general way. We are working towards a comprehensive account of human consciousness, and perhaps to a dramatic expansion of our own capabilities.

Because the field is so enormous—whole books have been written on single aspects of psychology, and even these have not been comprehensive—this volume will of necessity be limited and incomplete. But *Understanding Psychology* will offer an introduction to the fundamental concepts, a basis for wider exploration in the vast and exciting literature of psychology and, more particularly, the essential background for full appreciation of the more detailed discussions in the remaining volumes of the *Life Cycle* series.

Psychology and life

We are all psychologists of a kind. In our everyday lives we do what the psychologist does in the laboratory. We watch our fellow humans and listen to what they say. We observe how they react to what we do. We gather together the information from our observations and form theories (short people are aggressive; women are nervous drivers; long-haired students smoke pot). And we test these theories by watching to see if our predictions are accurate; or we seek out evidence to support them. Often we are wrong, although we do not readily admit it. Our common sense may be adequate for many tasks and situations, but it can also lead us to wrong conclusions and make our actions ineffective. Many of our ideas about human nature, personality, cultural

influences, may be simply prejudices or based on assumptions derived from our own natures, personalities and upbringing. We may be poor observers of phenomena, uncritical of information, inadequate assimilators of complex ideas; and this can lead us to misusing psychology, to 'psychologising'.

In attempting to understand or explain behaviour it is easy to become attached to false or oversimplified arguments in order to support our propositions. We say, to take a simple example, 'The violence evident in large, poor families is due to conditions of overcrowding.' Why? Because everyone knows that when lots of rats are placed in a small cage they will eventually turn on each other and even kill the weaker rats.

The idea is interesting, the inference tempting; but the assumptions are incorrect. It is true that *some* people will get violent and that others will become panic-stricken or riotous in overcrowded conditions; but *most* people will not. Even for those who do, there may be any number of other reasons for their apparently 'typical' behaviour. Rats do not equal humans do not equal entire races. Rats hoard, some gypsies hoard. Are the gypsies *all* misers? Will they kill their brethren in an overcrowded caravan site? No. Yet this process of simplifying the world we live in by making analogies between unlike things can dominate all our responses, even our way of life.

The more complex or baffling a situation, 'the greater our desire to simplify it. Psychologists shudder at this tendency. They argue that the more complexity we can cope with the better, if we are interested in the truth about ourselves and the way we

7

behave. The greater our maturity, the less we will need to simplify or psychologise and the better we will be able to accommodate ourselves to real life, which is not simple. This is why psychologists attempt to follow the methods of science.

Unravelling the mysteries

A hundred years ago the idea of adopting a scientific approach to the study of people was an exciting novelty. At that time it seemed great progress to discover how large the difference had to be between two weights for a person—any person—to be able to discern that difference. Then it was found that much the same was true in judging differences in loudness, colour or the length of lines. This was an important discovery: it carried the implication that human beings behave in regularly repeatable and predictable ways to which an experimental method of investigation is appropriate.

This development led directly to the next great advances, which come about by using scientific methods to try to answer the question: 'How do we become competent adults?' We start out as helpless infants: at least a part of the new behaviour acquired along the path of development to adulthood must be learned: how does the learning process operate?

Children who live with deadly danger (they are fleeing from bombardment) come to understand death and survival far earlier than might be expected from development theory.

The first scientific answers came from a Russian physiologist, Pavlov, and an American psychologist, Thorndike. They showed that learning depends on reward and punishment. But their discoveries were more subtle than is apparent from that statement. Just any reward, given at any time, will not do: it must be something that is really wanted by the organism at a *biological* level, and it must come very soon (about half a second) after the behaviour that is to be learned.

We now know that learning is in fact a more complicated process than that, but that was the simple seed from which a great deal of psychology grew. An important aspect of Pavlov and Thorndike's work was that they experimented with animals. With other pioneers, they were able to show that the learning of behaviour in humans can be reliably related to the same process in lower animals. This does *not* mean—as with the rats and the gypsies on page 7—that humans behave like animals, but that humans and animals *learn* some of their behavioural patterns in similar ways. In fact we humans have learned a great deal about ourselves by methodically investigating specific aspects of animal behaviour.

'Why am I climbing the mountain? Because it's there!' But the chimps only seem *to be behaving like humans.*

Psychology in this guise was known as 'the science of behaviour', or more fully, 'the science of the behaviour of organisms'. But an older definition was 'the science of mental life', and many modern psychologists are returning to this definition, which makes 'consciousness' a central concept and encourages the study of dreams, fantasy, memories, thought processes, sensations and so on—all aspects of the functioning of mind.

Earlier psychologists, particularly the early *behaviourists*, either denied the importance of such phenomena or saw them as special kinds of behaviour. They argued that, for example, thoughts may bear very little relation to what the thinker actually does or is. A man may regard himself as a lion, but be seen by his friends as a mouse, a mild, gentle chap with slightly ridiculous notions. According to the behaviourists, it is what he actually *does* which matters to others and, in the long run, to himself. Actions speak louder than words.

Psychology as a science

As a modern science, psychology has entered an exciting period in which discovery follows discovery. Research techniques have been steadily improving throughout this century and the results of many later psychological experiments have an authority and definition lacking in some early work. These results, incorporated into a body of theory, have also become more intelligible and more accessible, and as such can be of much greater use to every one of us.

Is psychology therefore the answer to our problems? Will it satisfactorily explain all our behaviour? Offer a means of 'curing' behaviour we call 'bad'? Open our minds? It is not quite as simple as that.

A rope of many strands

There are a surprising number of theories which guide psychological research and interpretation. Some of them were originally formulated in response to questions which seemed important at the time of their conception or which seemed to accord with prevailing philosophical ideas. For example, it is possible to assign the paternity of Freudian ideas as much to the intellectual and social climate of late Victorian Vienna as to the master's originality. The great Swiss psychologist Jean Piaget's work on intelligence may be seen to be ineradicably associated with the European rationalist intellectual tradition. The proliferation and wide acceptance of behaviourist theories is equally traceable to the dominance in the mid-20th century of American scientific ideas. Even the current interest in Eastern psychology is the concomitant of our contemporary fascination with self-awareness.

But the transience of the conditions in which theory is conceived need not affect the permanence of its validity or usefulness, any more than the fact that Mozart has been dead for nearly 200 years affects the meaning of *Don Giovanni*.

It is therefore not surprising that psychology is less simple a discipline than we might like it to be. Its pattern is intricately woven from such diverse theoretical strands as those which accord pre-eminence to cognitive processes, or to critical stages of development, or future goals and aspirations, or to social expectations and pressures, or to 'drives', or to 'here-and-now' phenomenology, or to being 'born that way', and so on. *Understanding Psychology* attempts to examine some of these strands and to show what strength each imparts to the fabric of psychology.

With so many different assumptions about human nature, it is naturally difficult to know exactly *what* needs to be investigated and explained. Each theory not only leads to its own questions but tends also to have its own preferred methodology, which may be different from all the others. This can and often does result in the findings associated with one viewpoint being only imperfectly compatible, or indeed in plain disagreement, with those of other viewpoints. Behaviour, that is to say, is not something that can be defined or understood with the precision of, for example, the workings of an automatic gearbox or even a computer. Nevertheless, a scientific psychology does provide both a frame of reference for, and many keys to, the interpretation of how humans behave.

'*Behaviour is not something that can be understood with the same precision as an automatic gearbox ...*'

In this introductory volume, we will examine some of the central areas of psychology as seen by a psychologist whose initial training has been in the behaviourist school and who salutes its importance to contemporary psychology. This approach concerns itself with the objective study of *observable* responses (activities, movements), which must also be *measurable*. Although there is considerable disagreement as to what constitutes 'behaviour' itself, most psychologists would agree that behaviour is *what an organism observably does*.

Understanding Psychology will not attempt a reconnaissance of the frontiers of psychological theory and practice, where exploration and discovery continue. It seeks to provide the kind of map that shows main roads, major stopping places and useful secondary routes for a drive through a large and settled country, rather than the kind of large-scale chart you would use to find your way on foot through a mile of rough woodland. That detailed exploration is for the volumes that make up the *Life Cycle* series.

These will cover such areas of outstanding human interest as the developmental process (the way a child grows into adulthood), ageing, pregnancy and family psychology, adolescence, interpersonal relationships, and such important phenomena as addictions, stress and anxiety, sexual behaviour and ethics. Some volumes will share the present emphasis on a behavioural approach; others will offer different standpoints. But all psychologists recognise the importance of the topics discussed in this volume, which is intended to illuminate some major viewpoints and discoveries of psychology. In order that progress from here to other more advanced works may be smooth and logical, the chapters are arranged under the traditional headings used in most major introductory texts.

Voodoo in Haiti: the psychological mechanism of mystical fervour has yet to be fully investigated.

The soft machine outlines the importance of the brain and of our senses—it is an introduction to physiological psychology and the mysteries of how our behaviour is controlled by what we call 'grey matter' located in the topmost part of our heads, and how behaviour is influenced by sense organs which never seem to fail us—but sometimes do.

We live and learn explains the process of learning and shows that

People in the audience have attitudinal 'sets': it is the orator's intention to change them. Both matters fall within the psychologist's field of study.

it is central to all behaviour. Without the ability to learn, we are quite unable to survive or develop as human beings.

Remembering and forgetting explores the way we store what we have learned. This chapter also offers practical advice on how to improve your memory.

In *Looking for a motive* and *Revealing our feelings* we turn to the forces, feelings and actions which direct our behaviour.

'*I am that I am*' looks at the concept of personality and how some psychologists 'bring it all together'. Personality, you will discover, means much more to psychologists than an open smile and a firm handclasp. This chapter also gives examples of how psychologists set about measuring personality.

In *Going off the rails* we consider some of the ways in which people fail to function adequately. Here we touch on psychological illness and what hope different therapies hold out for the mentally sick, or the behaviourally maladjusted.

Finally, in *Towards a better world*, we briefly examine the role psychology can play in the world of tomorrow and ask how psychology can contribute towards the qualitative improvement of the human race.

Psychology at your service

Psychology does not only relate to the world at large. It relates to individuals within their world and it can be applied to everyday life. But many—perhaps most—people simply do not know how this science of mind and behaviour can help them overcome or cope with the problems of their lives. Often this is because psychological knowledge is thought to reside only in difficult academic texts.

On the following pages, a question-and-answer method is used to provide guidelines to the heart of the matter.

What is the difference between psychoanalysts, psychiatrists and psychologists? Aren't they all 'mind doctors'?

The *psychoanalyst* believes in and practises psychoanalysis, the theories and methods developed from the work of Sigmund Freud and his disciples. This is a specific method of treating mental disorders by investigating and exploring the *unconscious* processes of the mind. The causes of the disorder, such as repressed childhood memories, are brought to the surface and identified as part of the therapeutic process. Psychoanalysts are often qualified doctors with additional training in analytic techniques. Most psychoanalysts have to undergo personal analysis as part of their training.

Psychiatry is a specific branch of the medical profession, 'mind doctors' if you like. All psychiatrists are qualified doctors. Psychiatry aims to prevent, assess and treat mental illnesses. As an extension of the medical profession, mainstream psychiatry tends to regard deviant or abnormal behaviour as the same kind of thing as we generally call 'mental disease'. But some would confine this term 'disease' to such conditions as schizophrenia. Methods of treatment vary according to the psychiatrist and the nature and extent of the patient's problems. Methods include psychotherapy, drug therapy, and, more rarely, electrotherapy.

These days it is not just child assessment (right) and rats in mazes: psychologists must also be administrators (above).

The main difference between psychiatrists and *clinical psychologists*—those who are trained to deal with 'sick' minds—is that psychiatrists are empowered to use drugs and electrotherapy in addition to psychotherapy, when trying to alter behaviour patterns or cure illnesses. Psychologists only make use of psychotherapy. Yet the psychologist draws on a much broader spectrum of study and experience as a basis of operations than does the psychiatrist. The psychologist will have studied the behaviour of animals and people in their *normal* and *abnormal* states, hoping to shed light on why organisms behave as they do in 'real life'.

What kinds of problems are psychologists supposed to help with?

As a profession, psychology's concern is the welfare of the human being. It assumes that healthy human beings make for a healthy society which in turn makes life enjoyable and rewarding. To achieve this, psychologists try to understand how and why people act as they do. There are at least 30 identifiable subdivisions within the practice of psychology, many of them now registered as distinct disciplines, each of them with a distinguished and jealously-maintained record of contributions to the whole field of psychology.

Would I be familiar with what psychologists do?

You are bound to have come across some of them. Psychologists work in schools, in counselling and guidance services; there are child, social, physiological, experimental, academic, industrial and personnel, vocational, engineering and space, military, psychotherapy and clinical psychologists. Psychologists are even being drawn into politics to give advice on issues ranging from racial discrimination and media violence to military strategy and urban living conditions.

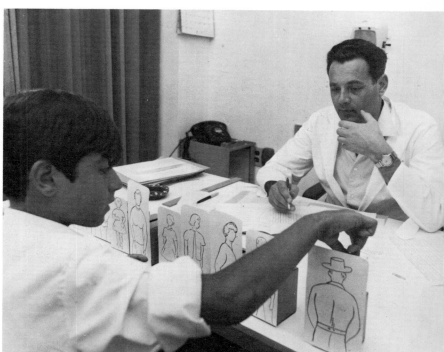

Thousands of experiments are performed around the world each year, in matters as various as what causes left-handedness, why you blink your eyelids, how addicts can be persuaded to give up drinking, smoking or drugs, what child-rearing patterns

Child observation is important not only in its own right but also for the insights it can offer into human behaviour generally.

promote effective and happy adults, how to prevent mental illnesses and/or behavioural disorders, how to promote effective cooperative living—almost every aspect of life can be investigated by psychologists: almost no problem is too remote from human behaviour for it to be of help.

In spite of its many different and apparently conflicting theories, in spite even of the number of untrained and sometimes dangerous 'quacks' who persist in attaching themselves to the name, psychology these days is just as much a recognised professional discipline as the law or medicine (and can overlap with both).

Do most psychologists work in clinics, with mentally sick people?

Clinical psychologists make up about one-third of the profession around the world. They have a long theoretical and practical training usually culminating in a hospital internship, and a Ph.D degree, which prepares them as diagnosticians, therapists and 'consultants' on a wide variety of issues. These may range from less serious adjustment problems, family tensions, marital conflicts and sexual problems to mental retardation, addiction and delinquency. More serious mental illnesses and behavioural disorders also fall within their province. Clinical psychologists work in, for example, mental hospitals, institutions for the old or

Social psychologists interest themselves in the formation, structure and behaviour of groups.

Jetliner controls are installed not just where they happen to fit but ergonomically—to match the way men function mentally and physically.

the mentally handicapped, and rehabilitation centres, or in private practice, perhaps with a team of professional colleagues. Nowadays, clinicians are moving into private practice on a much wider scale.

What about the non-clinical specialisations?

Social psychology is an important specialisation which studies individuals within their natural social and cultural settings. Social psychologists 'observe' behaviour as a main method of study and examination when investigating the psychological bases of social life. Most social psychologists work in academic or research institutions. Others help with market-research projects and advertising. Many also apply their scientific research findings to practical matters as for example when teaching social skills to those who seek to improve their interpersonal behaviour.

Educational psychologists are often attached to local education authorities or to child-guidance clinics or government agencies with school psychology services. They may act in an advisory capacity, or they may do research on projects to promote more effective education. These projects may cover subjects such as the most valuable use of visual aids or how to promote parent-teacher-child interaction. Educational psychologists apply their findings in various ways: they train school psychologists, teachers and social workers in guidance, counselling and therapy and also assist in the diagnosis and solution of a child's problems at home or in the classroom.

Could psychologists help me at work?

Once again, yes. *Industrial* psychologists are concerned with restoring the 'human' element in industry and finding ways of promoting greater efficiency. They conduct research on all aspects of work—job satisfaction, accident frequency, personnel selection, productivity and so on. They may organise training programmes to improve the quality and performance of individual workers, from the managing director to the shop-floor sweeper.

Engineering psychologists are even more specialised. They study the relationship between people and machines, with a view to designing machinery best suited to human functioning. This can range from helping to plan the instrument panel of a jumbo jet to improving the design of an electric light bulb fitment. You will come across such words as *ergonomics* (designed to match human characteristics) and *bio-engineering* (how best to mix men and machines) in their branch of the calling.

So psychology is not just one branch of say, 'learning' or 'personality', but covers everything we do?

It is possible to find a use for a psychologist in most aspects of life. There are, for instance, *occupational* psychologists who aim to get the best out of human resources in more practical and efficient ways. There are *experimental* psychologists who use precise scientific methods to investigate how individuals respond to the world around them. But in other areas of psychology, too, the method of experimentation (and the testing of hypotheses) is used. Thus *physiological* psychologists try to discover what they can about the association between the biological processes of mind and body and human behaviour.

But they can't all go about their work in the same way?

There are various approaches available to psychologists. For example, *neurophysiologists* originally discovered that specific areas of the brain produce different emotions like pain and pleasure. By repeatedly producing particular effects, neurophysiologists established the notion that human behaviour is controlled by the activity of the brain and neurons. This seems a satisfactory way to investigate specific aspects of human action, such as learning. However, it falls far short of explaining more complicated sequences.

Psychoanalysis is completely different. It is a complex body of theory based on observation; but it is speculative in its interpretations. Psychoanalysis regards much of our behaviour as influenced (even propelled) by a variety of desires or instincts buried deeply in our unconscious, of which we may be totally unaware. Psychoanalysts believe that the process of uncovering these unconscious feelings assists the individual towards a better understanding of his or her problems and helps psychological growth and fulfilment.

The *behavioural* approach can be described as falling between the above two methods. Behavioural psychologists are trained to observe behaviour in order to understand the human condition. Other people may be able to guess what you are feeling, but you alone have the conscious experience of your emotions. Other people have to rely on what you tell them. As this can often be misleading, trained observers use standardised criteria which help in the interpretation of behaviour.

This behavioural approach is often called stimulus (what you see)–response (your reaction to the message) psychology, or S–R for short. Behaviourists are more interested in stimuli and people's responses than what happens *inside* an individual. Behaviourists and analysts, although their approaches may sound superficially similar, differ in their acceptance of what constitutes 'data', in the way they obtain their findings and, especially, in their explanations of why and how people behave in certain ways.

Do these three approaches cover all possibilities?

No, there are others. *Existential* psychology, for example, maintains optimistically that people are 'free' to select and determine what they do, that people are responsible to themselves for every action. A powerful motivation towards 'self-fulfilment' drives us on as we seek to fulfil our potential in life in the best possible way. And the ultimate goal is the realisation of this potential. The *encounter-group* movement has its roots in existentialism.

Are these different approaches ever brought together?

Cognitive psychology combines some, if not all, of these approaches. In this context, 'cognitive' means the process by which we think about things, see them and know that they exist. Cognitivists argue that, as environmental stimuli hold our attention and affect our behaviour, we recall past experience. They aim to investigate the mental processes responsible for this recall. By breaking these down and examining the component parts, the overall picture of behaviour is more easily pieced together.

So the approach of behaviourists and analysts, say, would be different from cognitivists when faced with the same problem? Which would be right?

Towards an eclectic psychology: interchange of ideas between different 'schools' at a conference.

Psychologists of different persuasions will tackle the whole variety of human problems with the best of their own traditional knowledge. Many psychologists do not keep to one particular school of thought. They adapt their methods of approach according to the kind of problem they are dealing with. This is known as *eclectic* psychology. Here, assumptions, theories and levels of analysis and treatment are used to suit the occasion, rather than allowing any one line of approach to predominate. It is impossible to say which is right in general terms. You can only go by results—and the results may be 'good' or 'bad', entirely depending on the criteria adopted by the practitioner or researcher.

How would I set about finding the right psychologist for my own problems?

A cardinal rule must be: ensure that your psychologist is properly trained and has legitimate accreditation. Once this is established, it is always wise to choose a psychologist whose approach you agree with and approve of. You should ensure that his or her knowledge covers the area your problem falls into, and that he or she is someone whom you find agreeable, otherwise there can be little chance of a productive outcome.

But if there are so many different kinds of psychologists, many of them disagreeing with one another, how can psychology be a single, effective discipline?

There is an overriding commitment by all psychologists to professional methods and purposes held in common by all branches—description, explanation, understanding, interpretation, prediction, and control. These steps in the process of understanding and developing the human mind and body are continually applied in the search to improve the quality of all our lives—the ultimate objective of psychology and psychologists everywhere.

2 The soft machine

In and out, in and out goes our breath, and 'lup-dup, lup-dup' beat our hearts, whether we are awake or asleep, thinking about ourselves or not. We do not have to instruct our eyes to blink when a bright light flashes, or concentrate on scratching our noses when they itch. But when we drive, or write books called Understanding Psychology, *or cook a soufflé, all the actions connected with those things have to be under precise conscious control. Even so, our performance may be graceful and efficient, or clumsy and blundering, without our being able to do very much to change it. All in all, we could be forgiven for believing that quite different kinds of activity were going on in us.*

But in reality all are merely different manifestations of the working of a single, integrated system—woodwind or string passages, as it were, in the intricately orchestrated harmony of our immense physiological resources.

The state of our being

William Burroughs used a neat and useful phrase to describe the human body—'the soft machine'.[1] But if we are machines, then those machines are of staggering ingenuity and complexity. The financial, political and cultural, welfare, military and industrial organisation of a vast and successful nation-state would seem crudely inefficient, elementary in its workings, beside the information and control systems needed to keep the body and mind of any one of that country's citizens functioning normally.

Although psychology as a science is not wholly dependent on physiology, an understanding of human behaviour must take into account the control systems of 'the soft machine'. Each of these two sciences produces its own explanations of behaviour—psychological and physiological. But each science gains from familiarity with the other. Some of the findings and formulations of physiology covered in this chapter will prove useful for a better understanding of the purely psychological discussions that follow.

The god in the machine?

The brain contains 11 billion or so cells, called *neurons*, organised into interconnecting networks. Of course not all of them are in use at any one time—indeed a great many brain cells seem never

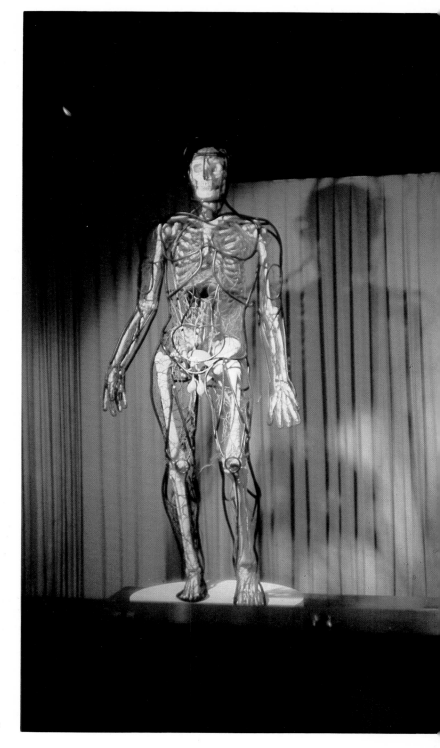

*'The intricately
orchestrated harmony
of our immense
physiological resources.'*

21

to be used at all. No one ever exploits all of his or her brain, and nobody has yet satisfactorily explained why it should be so complicated, why we appear to have been endowed with this super-abundance of brain capacity. Perhaps some day we will learn how to use this great reserve of what is, after all, our most important resource.

Would we all be Uri Gellers if we had access to the full resources of our brains?

Yet it is not only the brain that controls and moulds our behaviour and experience. Neurons pass down our spinal column to form the *autonomic system*, which controls various muscle complexes and glands. This autonomic nervous system (ANS) keeps us in good shape, moderates the heart beat and our skin temperature. At appropriate times it also prepares us for 'fight or flight' by signalling for the release of adrenalin and for other changes from our 'normal' or resting state. The way these systems interact with each other largely determines the physiological component of behaviour.

'Stop' means all systems go!

Consider a 'simple' sequence. You are driving through town, the traffic lights change to red, and you bring your car to a halt. What actually happens during those few seconds? Your eyes, while scanning the road ahead, are attracted by the 'red light' pattern. Electrical excitation travelling from the retina of the eye back into the brain (where you find what we might call the Vision Control Centre) is accompanied by chemical changes. The stimulus—red light—is checked for meaning, broken down and compared with your experience of 'red lights' stored in your memory. Red lights can signify more than 'stop'. But in this case the brain recognises a particular, familiar command and sets off a programme of learned behaviour.

Perhaps your first reaction is to consider (with lightning rapidity) whether or not you can beat the lights, break the law and avoid hitting any cross traffic. This appraisal and its outcome will be shaped by previous experience: knowledge of the road, your abilities as a driver, the capacity of your car, your views on driving and the law.

All systems stop!

23

Present perception also plays a part: are there pedestrians or police constables about? How close is any following traffic? Is that a sports car or a hearse waiting to cross your path? And how are you feeling: relaxed or tense, happy or angry? Are you in a hurry or just taking it easy? Do you really want to take a risk? Face possible death or delicensing? And how will others in the immediate vicinity respond to your actions?

This time, the sum of your judgments is that you should obey the signal. Your foot leaves the accelerator and moves to the brake. So far the whole process has been smooth and rapid. Thousands of neurons have 'fired', messages have flashed through your head and body. In total, they may have travelled *further than the full distance of your journey.* Your body has tensed a little, hands are gripping the steering wheel rather more firmly, muscles in the lower trunk, legs and feet are at work in order to ensure the exact amount of pressure.

At this stage, other senses are coming into play. The eyes are still feeding information to the brain, but the sense of balance (the *vestibular sense*) is reporting on the sensation of deceleration. The muscles themselves are 'feeding back' information. Decisions are being taken. Is it necessary to increase pressure on the brake? Or to ease off a little? Is it time to change gear? And you thought driving was simple . . ..

To stand with them, speed of perception— and reaction—have to be exceptional.

A whole book could be written on the psychology and physiology of this particular sequence (or almost any other: just imagine what is involved in playing the violin!). And then another volume on the decision to 'chance it' and attempt to beat the lights.

This second volume would pay considerable attention to the autonomic nervous system and its role in directing the *endocrine glands* to pump adrenalin. The heart rate would increase as would the rate of breathing; the general body condition would change in gross and subtle ways. You might experience fear or anxiety followed by relief or elation. 'Emergency' brings forth a dramatic speeding up of the physiological process.

With all this, the question of neural transmission—*how* messages and impulses are passed around the brain and body— has not yet been taken into consideration. But the example gives some small insight into the elaborate components of a single act we tend to take for granted—the bringing of a car to a halt. Recognise that at least this degree of physiological activity accompanies everything that you do, every day, and the spectacle of the soft machine becomes overwhelming, indeed miraculous.

Many people assume that science 'explains away' the marvellous and mysterious. This is simply not so. To journey into science is to discover wonders around every corner.

Even under very high physical stresses, the co-ordination of the body's electric, chemical and mechanical functions is remarkable.

The mysteries of the organism

In partnership with their peers in the medical, biological and behavioural sciences, psychophysiologists are drawing a more coherent picture of our inner scenery, focusing on the central nervous system (CNS) and the autonomic nervous system (ANS). This century has seen the systematic exploration of the neural pathways that lead to and from the brain, and an unravelling of the secrets of the great communications cable that descends the spinal column through rings of vertebrae into ever smaller interconnecting networks. In the past few decades alone, psychophysiologists have begun to crack the mysteries of both nerve-cell structure and the vast neuronal network that stretches for miles throughout our bodies. They have tracked individual nerve impulses and followed the chemical messages which can speed information through the countless cells in the average human body.

A closer look at the neuron

The human brain contains between 10 and 12 billion of the basic cells called *neurons*, vital to functions directly responsible for our behaviour and experience. Although some neurons are highly specialised, all of them share the same three-part structure. There is the *cell body* from which sprout short fibres called *dendrites* and a longer nerve fibre called the *axon*.

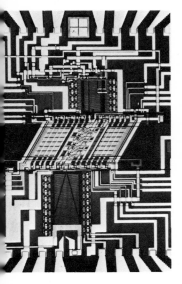

The nearest we have got to making something like our brain matter—the 'silicon chip' or microprocessor.

The neuron is essentially a system for transmitting information in the form of a *nerve impulse*. Such impulses are picked up by one or more dendrites and then passed by the cell body along the axon to be further transmitted to the dendrites of other nerve cells and finally to the activating 'relays' of particular muscles or glands.

Neurons handle one-way traffic only. Impulses can be initiated only at the dendrite and carried from there to the end of the axon. The axon may be as little as one micron (one-thousandth of a millimetre) in diameter, and can range in length from 1 mm to as much as 2 metres.

How the nerve impulse is transmitted

We now think we know that the process is *electrochemical* in nature. A crude analogy to nerve action is a burning fuse—a flame applied to one end of the fuse gradually creeps to the other end. But an axon is not consumed by the passage of the 'flame': it can be re-used time and again; and it carries its excitation from one end to the other infinitely more rapidly than any fuse.

The neuron obeys an 'all or nothing' rule. It either *fires* or it does not. But the amount of energy necessary to set off the response depends on the neuron's size, your own physical condition and other factors: tiredness, lack of oxygen, drugs, can all inhibit the neuron and reduce its tendency to respond. Once fired, by electrically charged particles called *ions*, it transmits its message.

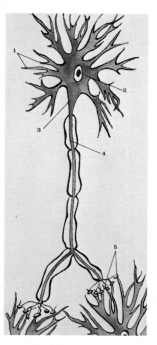

1 *dendrites*
2 *nucleus*
3 *cell body*
4 *axon*
5 *synaptic knobs*

We now have to ask what initiates this whole process in any particular neuron: what makes it respond in the first place? The same answer applies to all neurons, be they large, small, *sensory* (carrying impulses from the senses to the nervous systems), or *motor* (carrying impulses from the nervous system to the muscles). Each axon comes close to, but *never touches*, the dendrite of another neuron. The space between the end of an axon and the dendrite of the next neuron in the transmission line is called the *synaptic gap* or *synapse*.

Although the synapse separates the end of one neuron from the beginning of the other it is, at the same time, the connection between them, and the nerve impulse must act across it. When *synaptic transmission* takes place the electrical field generated by the firing of one neuron must be powerful enough to extend across the synapse and set off a reaction in the next neuron. The electrical field itself seems also to have a chemical component: it is almost as if the impulse shoots minute chemical particles across the gap. In spite of voluminous research done in this field in the past 20 years, there is still no complete explanation of how this occurs.

Pathways of discovery

There is much that still awaits to be discovered by physiologists, and quite simple questions still continue to tantalise them. We know a good deal about the chemistry of nerve fibres and about the dynamics of nerve impulses, for example, but we still have to explain how physical stimuli from the external world (light waves, changes in temperature) are converted into nerve impulses. An even greater mystery is how a particular impulse is routed through a single one of the almost infinite number of possible tracks available in the nervous system.

If we step back from this tight focus on the nerve mechanism, even larger questions come into view. How, for instance, does the system we have been considering cope with such daunting processes as selecting a life partner, learning a second language or writing a book?

All in the brain?

Psychophysiologists regard the brain as the 'encyclopaedia' in which most of the answers about behaviour are to be found. It is the device that makes us distinctly human (as opposed to animal—although many would argue we behave in much the same way as animals). It is an elaborate structure of quite amazing complexity and versatility.

The brain itself weighs about three pounds and is symmetrically divided into two hemispheres, left and right. We do not yet know why, but the left part of the brain controls the right side of the body and the right part controls the left side of the body. The hemispheres are connected by a large bundle of nerves which act as the communications channels between the regions of the brain.

The structure of the brain

The hindbrain controls all the normal bodily activities such as heartbeat, breathing, muscle co-ordination, posture, balance and so on, as well as the communications between our sense organs and limbs. The *midbrain* oversees all visual input and how it relates to our body's position. It also arouses a quiescent organism to respond to a threatening environmental stimulus. The *forebrain* is responsible for our sexual activities, our emotions, needs and

The midbrain at work: threat on one side brings 'flight-or-fight' response on the other.

drives. Mental functioning, such as thought processes, perception and speech, are also linked to this area of the brain.

The brain structure is clearly delineated and its functions have been carefully described. But some fascinating research on what happens to our behaviour when the two sides of the brain are surgically disconnected not only highlights the complexity of our so called 'grey matter' but underlines the old adage, 'the more we find out, the less we know'.

Split brains—double minds

It is now an established fact that both animals and we humans have split brains or, put differently, double minds. It is almost as though the same body were inhabited by two independent brains, each capable of performing all things separately. Although we may have learned to draw pictures with our right hand, we can draw pictures (less well) with our left hand too. We need not commence the learning-to-draw process anew when using our non-practised hand. In fact children often switch their pencils from hand to hand when first learning to draw. This implies that information stored in one hemisphere is also stored in the other hemisphere.

Were the two hemispheres to be disconnected from each other, we should lose our ability to integrate sensations from opposite sides of the body. Nor would we be able to co-ordinate our limb movements on both sides. Typically, if someone with a surgically

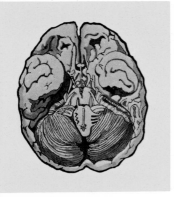

The human brain. View from underneath.

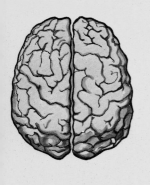

The human brain.
View from above.

split brain (rarely encountered) were touched on the right leg, he or she would not be able to point to that spot with the left hand. Pointing can only be done with the same side hand. The conclusion must be that each hemisphere can perform these functions separately; but that it does not inform the other side what it is capable of doing.

Another curious yet unexplained phenomenon is that, although each of the split hemispheres has 'normal' emotions, these emotions can simultaneously differ in each hemisphere. Many years ago, a psychologist named Holden reported the case of a split-brain man who, when extremely angry with his wife, grabbed her with his left hand and started shaking her violently, only to find his right hand intervening in an attempt to prevent him from doing so.[2]

Getting the messages through the networks

The brain itself is not an isolated organ but part—if the major and dominant part—of the *nervous system*. We know that the nervous system integrates and co-ordinates the neurons, enabling the different parts and systems of the body to 'talk' to each other. This all-important system is made up of two different yet closely connected structures.

The *central nervous system* (CNS) is housed in the skull and the spinal cord. Its primary function is to ensure that all parts of the body work together: it organises and integrates the person as a whole and is the seat of consciousness. The *peripheral nervous system* is formed by nerve fibres which connect the CNS to various *receptors* (which are sensitive to the external environment) and *effectors* (the various muscles and glands which ensure adequate physical adjustment to the external environment). The peripheral system itself breaks down into two further subsections, the *somatic* system and the *autonomic* system—which itself breaks

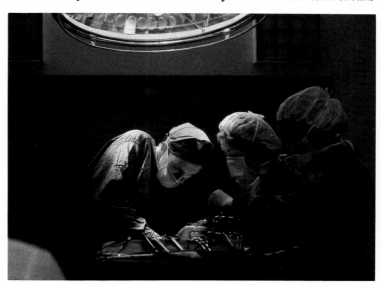

A matter of life and death—and all the body's physiological powers are focused on the scalpel's edge.

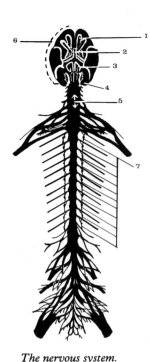

The nervous system.
1 olfactory bulb
2 pituitary body
3 pons
4 cerebellum
5 spinal cord
6 cerebrum
  (right hemisphere)
7 nerve 'skeleton'
  of the autonomic
  system

down further into two very important functional systems, the *sympathetic* and *parasympathetic*.

These are situated at different points along the brain stem and spinal cord. The sympathetic system nestles into the middle of the spinal cord (between the neck and spinal cord) while the parasympathetic system ties in above and below the sympathetic nerve fibres (hence *para*, which means 'next to').

The sympathetic division is like a general in the battlefield, marshalling his troops in times of an emergency. It operates when life is threatened, or when we feel intense emotions such as rage, anger, fear or even when we are physically exerting ourselves quite strenuously. In other words, it prepares the organism for action—increases heart rate, stimulates adrenalin flow, sees that blood is diverted to the muscles, stops the liver from using sugar which the muscles will need, and so on.

The parasympathetic system is like the army's quarter-master, keeping the troops in good shape by tending to their vital needs. It is responsible for the conservation of bodily energy, digestion, elimination of waste products, the protection of our sensory systems and the general maintenance of balance in the organism as a whole.

Checks and balances
The maintenance of a balance in all these activities is achieved by a form of antagonistic cooperation between the sympathetic and parasympathetic systems—they work *against* each other. If the former begins to stimulate the organism into greater activity, the latter restrains it, or at least dampens the overall effect in order to stop the organism from 'going wild' with all its systems running berserk. Man's sexual response illustrates the point well. When sexually aroused, a man will first have an erection (a parasympathetic function) followed by ejaculation (a sympathetic function) to stop the arousal process.

Feedback
Western physiologists assumed until recently that the body functions controlled by the autonomic nervous system were beyond conscious control. The heart rate and blood pressure, for example, were seen as varying, but only as a result of changes in the internal or external environment, not at our conscious command. There is some validity in this assumption for practical purposes—and indeed the two kinds of function, 'voluntary' and 'involuntary', are related to different kinds of operating muscle, 'striped' or 'smooth'. But it is not always true.

This chapter opened with the thought that although we are aware of many of our behavioural acts others occur without any conscious control, like scratching one's head over a difficult problem whilst simultaneously screwing up one's face in a contorted way. Until someone else points it out to you, you will be totally unaware of such chunks of behaviour. Once told however, you might catch yourself about to embark on the head-scratching, face-contorting routine and avoid it. *Awareness precedes control*. This is the watchword of a relatively newly-explored phenomenon called *biofeedback*, a procedure which allows us to monitor and even change the so-called 'involuntary' physiological processes.

Plumbing the body's secrets

In biofeedback experiments, tiny changes which take place in the brain or the body are detected, amplified and shown to the participant and/or researcher. Computer technology enables the person to 'tune in' to his or her inside world—heart-rate changes, blood pressure, temperature variations and brain-wave patterns. These biological processes, ordinarily undetectable by the person in whom they are occurring, offer *feedback* or knowledge to the participant. Typically a 'goal' is set up—such as 'let's alter your blood pressure please'—following which the person gauges his or her progress towards the specified goal. Research has shown that blood pressure can be dropped by as much as 15 per cent, skin temperature changes by up to 9°F, and heartbeat rates by as much as 35 beats per minute. Thus the arcane processes of the body which have, of course, always been available as working data to the hidden brain can now be brought out into the light of consciousness, to the same senses by which we perceive the outside world.

Connections with the world

Traditionally we have always spoken of the five senses: vision, hearing, touch, smell and taste. Psychologists add a further two to the list—body movement and balance. The senses themselves are not unitary, but combinations of elements with which most of us are familiar—taste (based on bitter, sweet, sour and salt) or touch (whose elements are cold, warmth, pressure and pain). All experience through these senses comes from different combinations of those components.

Our senses are continuously interacting: just think of what is involved in cooking even a simple meal—tasting the soup, smelling the pie burning, using your free hand to turn down the gas under the pan you are watching and listening to the beans boil over, all simultaneously! If you are more ambitious, there will be an even plainer demonstration of sense interaction when you come to test whether your soufflé is done—do you smell it just about to burn while you prod its side with a skewer and see if the top is too brown?

Blind people 'see' the world around them through their senses. They use touch to 'read' Braille and 'see' in busy city streets through a well-developed sense of movement and balance. How they navigate their way around remains unclear, although an interesting clue can be gleaned from bats. Bats live without vision in total darkness. As they fly around they emit a curious sound which reflects back off objects in the environment—like echoes.

Even with the help of a guide dog the blind man uses his cane to find his way. He listens to the echoes of its tapping— a kind of sonar *feedback.*

This kind of feedback is called *sonar* information, and has technological equivalents in echo-sounding depth recorders and submarine detection equipment, and an analogy with radar.

In an interesting experiment designed to test whether this ability could be found in humans, W. Kellog[3] found that blind people were able to differentiate between the textures of various cloths covering certain objects better than sighted people wearing blindfolds. Kellog asked all subjects to emit noises that produced echoes from the surrounding environment. When doing this, blind people performed significantly better than their sighted peers.

How do the senses work?

Our senses have a common property known as *threshold*. A sound must be loud enough to break our 'threshold of hearing' before we actually experience hearing itself. Below a particular level of intensity we hear nothing. (This is much the same as the way the neurons themselves operate—there has to be a significant input before they will fire.) Were this not so, our lives would be a torment of confused but unimportant stimuli clamouring for attention: there would be a danger that we could not sort out the significant from the insignificant. For this reason we seem to be able to adapt our thresholds to our environmental needs. As you read these words, you are probably unaware of the slight noise the central heating system may be making. Nor will you sense the pressure of your watch-strap on your skin. If someone turns off the central heating, you will at that very moment (and slightly beyond) hear and register the *difference*. That ability might be very important in, say, threatening situations. The ambiance changes, you notice the new soundless situation; but you will quickly adapt to it if it is of no significance.

Non-sense

It is often said of someone whose behaviour is bizarre that 'he has lost his senses'. There is a kernel of truth there, as Donald Hebb discovered in a now classic experiment.[4] Student volunteers were paid to lie passively on a bed in a laboratory and experience as little sensation as possible. This was effected by each volunteer having to wear a face mask, gloves, arm cuffs, and being swathed in cotton wool. Background noise was held constant (the sound of an air conditioner). The volunteers were allowed to eat and go to the bathroom only when necessary. Otherwise they lay quite still during 24 hours of each day.

Hebb's findings were quite riveting. At first the students enjoyed the experience—actually getting paid to catch up on some well-earned sleep! But sleeping soon turned into waking, boredom set in, and later the volunteers uniformly entered a phase of vivid hallucination. Some would hear things, others would see things, and still others would report feeling things. None of these 'things' actually existed. It was almost as though the volunteers had to manufacture something out of nothing in order to maintain their sanity.

As Hebb's experiment suggests, when we are deprived of sensory experience from the environment around us, internal regulators begin to take over. Internal stimuli are very important in bringing about different reactions to the same external situation. How often have you reached out to don a sweater just as someone else stands up and opens a window because he or she is 'too hot'? Inner stimuli are closely linked to our reservoir of interests, attitudes, and motives, which attends and even shapes our behaviour in common situations.

Mental set is a phenomenon which emphasises the point well: we often see or hear only what we expect to see or hear in a given situation. Generally speaking, mothers have a mental set to hear their babies cry at night; they expect it to happen and wake up at the slightest sound. Yet these same mothers may well sleep right through the din of an alarm clock sounding off. Mental set often becomes a habit—as when the rustle of a curtain in the dead of night is constantly mistaken for an intruding burglar.

Seeing is not necessarily believing

We perceive things that are not there, we distort observed phenomena and, even more surprisingly, we are *all* guilty of illusions—that is, seeing things differently from the way they actually are. We may all think we are right, but we can be completely wrong. Here are some prime examples of the way in which most of us make sense out of some exceptional visual illusions. It must be said that psychologists have learned a great deal from such anomalies, the gist of which remains very comforting. We see, sense and interpret the world around us in a well ordered and highly organised manner.

Visual distortions and illusions

Here are some visual illusions and distortions which many of us may have come across at one time or another. They demonstrate how the eyes and brain, or both, often add bits and pieces of information to what is actually there to be seen. Most of these 'tricks' are easily explained but some of them remain perplexing. Are you doing the distorting or are the figures themselves helping you? Try to figure out what is happening.

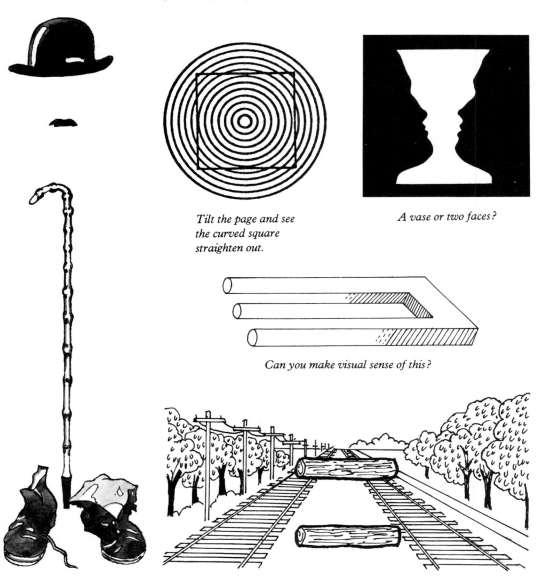

Tilt the page and see the curved square straighten out.

A vase or two faces?

Can you make visual sense of this?

Charlie Chaplin?

Which log would you prefer to lift?

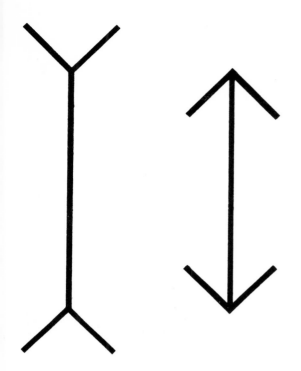

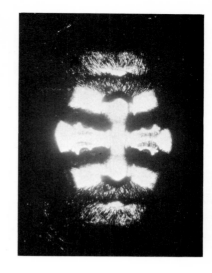

Which line is longer? Measure them and see.

Walk tall, David, you're bigger than Goliath—or are you?

3　We live and learn

The word 'learning' conjures images of conscientious students pouring over textbooks under the watchful eye of a tutor in a determined quest for knowledge. We are unlikely to think of it in terms of an unborn child, or of an old person rocking quietly in the shadows of life. But to the psychologist, learning is a lifelong process. From the time the human organism starts responding to touch and begins to recognise temperature change as an eight-week-old foetus, learning continues, as unceasingly as the heartbeat, until it dies, perhaps 80 or 100 years later.

A lifetime of lessons

In the first few years of this awesome pursuit of 'know-how' we are at a peak of our absorptive ability. We shuffle and crawl, then totter on two legs. In no time at all, we learn to run and jump and shriek at the sheer joy of it all. We discover how to co-ordinate larynx, lungs and tongue in order to make sounds, and we accommodate ourselves to the vocabulary and grammar of our spoken language—perhaps our most sophisticated achievement.

Young children first learn how to think in concrete terms. They classify objects in binary fashion—big, little; fat, thin; fast, slow; good, bad. A young child watching *Tom and Jerry* on television sees two cats and two mice: Big Tom and Little Tom, Big Jerry and Little Jerry. Perspective and its meanings have to be learnt.

During the desk-bound interlude in the classroom, we are formally instructed on matters that society decrees will be useful to us—or to society itself. But learning does not cease with a graduation ceremony. We constantly gain new information, discarding established views and seeking in other directions.

Without learning, life would be a relentless series of steps into the unknown. We would be confused, incapable of forming social relationships, growing or even preparing food. Along with memory, learning allows us to locate ourselves in time, to make order out of chaos, to survive.

The psychologists' use of the word 'learning' therefore applies to a far wider range of activities than common interpretation of the word allows. And psychology has a simple definition of the term which covers this wide range: *learning is the modification of behaviour as a result of experience.* This definition is good because it reveals the importance of day-to-day adaptation to events. Yet it is deceptively simple because it makes no attempt to *explain* learning and how it takes place. To grasp the scientific explanation

*Experience is
the best teacher.*

of learning, we must step back to the turn of the century and become acquainted with the work of a pioneer physiologist, the Russian Ivan Pavlov.

Pavlov and the conditioned response

Nobel Prizewinner Ivan Pavlov was one of the great founding fathers of scientific psychology. As a physiologist, he worked on the formation of patterns of association by studying the process of salivation in dogs when they were fed.[1] This is a straightforward *stimulus–response* situation. The dogs were kept hungry for specified periods of time, then fed by having food powder blown into their mouths. The amount of saliva they produced in response to this treatment could be measured and related to the degree of their hunger.

Here—and it complicated his original experiment—Pavlov made a key observation which was to lead him into a new area of research and finally to the formulation of influential theories which linked physiology, learning and personality. The observation was commonplace enough: the dogs often salivated *before* they were fed. It was Pavlov's tireless exploration of this phenomenon that earned him his place in history.

What he noticed was that the dogs *anticipated* food when they saw their keepers arriving with the feeding equipment. This is an associative process that we all know well. Our mouths water when we see lemons, for instance: maybe just reading the word 'lemon' or making a mental image of the fruit is enough to set off the mouth-watering response. Pavlov called the process *conditioning*. Today, out of respect for the physiologist's painstaking work on this basic learning process, we refer to it as *classical* or *Pavlovian conditioning*.

The most powerful weapon in the demagogue's armoury is conditioning: *standard response unfailingly following standard stimulus.*

After his initial observation that dogs would salivate in response to the sight of food, or even of the keepers who supplied them with it, Pavlov began introducing variations into his experimental scheme. He found that if feeding was always accompanied by the sound of a tuning fork, the dogs would learn to salivate to the tuning fork alone: they would become *conditioned* to the noise. He introduced careful definitions to distinguish between these phenomena. Food was the *unconditioned* stimulus, salivation when food was given an *unconditioned response*; the sound of tuning fork became the *conditioned stimulus* and salivation consequent on that sound the *conditioned response*.

Pavlov showed that for conditioning to take place the period of time between the conditioned stimulus (the tuning fork sound) and the delivery of food was critical. If too long a time elapsed, conditioning did not take place. He also studied *stimulus generalisation*. Having conditioned a dog to one note, he measured its conditioned response (its salivation) to other, different notes. As one would expect, notes that were close to the original produced salivation; the less alike were the two notes, the less likely would the second one be to produce a conditioned response.

Albert and the white rat

Some years after the publication of Pavlov's first experimental studies of conditioning, John B. Watson, a professor of psychology at Harvard, applied the principles of classical conditioning to a young child.[2] Albert was a happy 11-month-old who displayed no fear when shown a white rabbit, a white rat, a white fur coat, a white hairy mask—they were all *neutral stimuli*. But, like all children, Albert produced a 'startle' pattern, followed by fear, when a loud noise was made by striking an iron bar with a hammer. Watson showed that fear can be learned or conditioned and how, because of stimulus generalisation, fear can spread from fear of one object to fear of many.

Generalisation: having heard the word 'dead' while seeing (maybe on television) somebody lying still, the child takes 'Lie down you're dead' as a package.

Watson took the loud noise (unconditioned stimulus) and paired it with the rat (conditioned stimulus). After a few repeats of first being shown the rat and then being alarmed by the bar being struck, Albert became conditioned and showed fear (conditioned response) to the rat. Watson showed that the

conditioned fear response became generalised to other white, furry objects: the hairy mask, the rabbit, the fur coat. It should be made clear that there was no more conscious reasoning involved in Albert's conditioning than in that of Pavlov's dogs. Given the correct conditions—especially the correct period of time between the conditioned and unconditioned stimuli—conditioning takes place.

Extinction

The learned, or conditioned, response need not become fixed and permanent, but can gradually fade. Pavlov had already studied this phenomenon. He discovered that if he stopped presenting food after the sound of the tone, the sound gradually lost its effect on the dogs. A previously conditioned dog no longer associated the sound with the arrival of food and the conditioned response gradually died out. Pavlov called this effect *extinction*. By repeatedly presenting young Albert with the rat and *not* sounding the metal bar, Watson would have been able to decondition the child. Unfortunately—both for Albert and Watson's experiment—the child was removed from the experiment before extinction could be achieved. Whatever we may think of the propriety of subjecting a baby to this sort of experience (and I personally find it distasteful), Watson's work has had lasting importance in the study of conditioning.

Rewards and punishments

Giving in to tantrums will not stop them.

A second type of conditioning is based on the principle that rewarding—or *reinforcing*—certain behaviour encourages its repetition. Similarly, the absence of reward or the use of punishment tends to decrease the probability of behaviour being repeated. This learning from consequences is known by psychologists as *operant* or *instrumental* conditioning. B. F. Skinner is the name most closely associated with operant conditioning.[3] The controversial Harvard psychologist and his colleagues have shown time and again that most behaviour is related to the rewards and punishments it has produced in the past.

Take the child who is rewarded for being pleasing and charming—and compare her with her contemporary, who gets her way by being obnoxious and throwing temper tantrums. The parent of the second child tends to yield to aggressive behaviour 'for peace', thus rewarding her by giving in to her demands. A 'learned' pattern of behaviour is being set up—it can last well into adulthood.

We are all familiar with the application of operant conditioning in the animal world. The circus animal act is evidence enough. Here the elephant, say, is consistently rewarded for his antics with a loaf of bread; the seal receives a fish as a reward for a balancing trick, prancing horses a lump of sugar for their performance. This technique is applied in countless experimental situations in psychology laboratories throughout the world.

One psychologist, Verhave,[4] used it to train pigeons for a job in a pharmaceutical factory—and risked losing hundreds of men their jobs. He wanted to substitute pigeons for humans on an assembly line, picking defective capsules, or 'skags', off a conveyor belt. The pigeons were trained to peer through a small window at the capsules passing by on the belt at a rate of two each second. If they pecked a disc when a 'skag' came by, they were immediately rewarded. After only one week of this *positive reinforcement* for every correct peck, the pigeons were able to sort out 99 per cent of all the faulty capsules that moved along the conveyor belt. The men kept their jobs, but the birds proved a point, one which (as we shall see) has been adapted in various ways to improve both behavioural and work situations.

Withholding rewards

It is not necessary for every response to be reinforced for learning to take place. Indeed, one of the most valuable and striking results of research on learning is the discovery of different schedules. If a pigeon in an experiment is rewarded only every five minutes—the *fixed interval schedule*—instead of every time he makes the wanted response, then he will make that response more frequently. If you reward him sometimes after one minute, sometimes after three, sometimes after five and so on (this is called a *variable interval schedule*), he will respond faster than if you reward every response—but not as fast as on a fixed interval schedule. His response, however, will be more resistant to extinction—he will go on making it for longer in the hope of a reward because he is not certain when the next reward will come. A *fixed ratio* of reinforcement produces a higher rate of response (when you reinforce after a certain regular number of responses) and a *variable ratio* the highest of all.

This may explain the 'spoilt-child' response to adversity or difficulty. A person who has received everything he wanted all his life has very little protection when he meets his first frustration and defeat. He may give up on the spot. But one who has rarely received his heart's desires will be less frustrated when there are long gaps between success. He keeps plugging away until he succeeds.

Secondary reinforcers also make it possible to spread out rewards. If you shine a green light every time you reward an animal in an experiment, then the light and the reward become 'paired'. Soon the animal responds as much for the 'reward' of the light as it did previously for the real reward of food, sex, escape or whatever it was. This may look like cheating, but it is a development essential to the conduct of societies: most human life depends on secondary reinforcers. It would be a difficult world if we had to have a bite of food, a glass of beer or a kiss every time we performed satisfactorily. Instead we make do with one of the greatest secondary reinforcers of our time—money. A piece of paper or disc of metal has no value in itself, but we often work strenuously to get them—simply because we can then use them to acquire primary reinforcers of our own choice.

Token economy

It is much easier to devise and use operant conditioning techniques in shaping animals' behaviour than it is with humans. The range of possible behaviour is much smaller in animals and it is easier to control their total environment. For example, when food is used as a reinforcer, its effectiveness is usually guaranteed if the animals are kept permanently hungry—about ten per cent. underweight. Such control is rarely possible in experiments on humans.

None the less, the principles of operant conditioning have been used effectively to improve a wide range of human behaviours. The technique has been used as a form of therapy in mental hospitals, where the environment is restricted. Rewards in the form of tokens to be exchanged for various 'privileges' are awarded for improved behaviour—for instance, when a patient feeds himself, or goes to the toilet independently. The accumulation of a certain number of tokens allows a patient to eat his favourite food, visit relatives over a weekend, or watch television. Through inducements such as these, conditioning has scored some notable successes in mental and rehabilitation institutions, schools and classrooms, and even in industry.

The psychologist Ed Padelino used a novel form of the *token economy* to solve a chronic absenteeism problem in a factory.[5] Every morning, each man who arrived on time was dealt a playing card. At the end of the week, if he had been on time each morning, he had a complete poker hand. The factory was divided up into card 'schools'. They did not actually play, but the man with the best hand in each school was awarded a bonus. Absenteeism immediately dropped by a third, and stayed down. Although highly successful in this specific instance, such techniques could not be expected to be effective in all or even many problems of industrial relations. (See *Motivation at Work* in Chapter 5.)

Such behavioural techniques are popular and effective tools in the difficult business of child-rearing. Indeed, so confident are some psychologists—like Azrin and Foxx—that they claim that, with the aid of their methods, mothers can toilet train their children in a day.[6] But nothing is free: for that day the mother must attend to her child's *every move and action*.

Learning to learn

Harry Harlow made a significant contribution to our knowledge of the learning process by showing how animals can 'learn how to learn'.[7] He put two lids—one red, the other green—in front of a monkey. The green lid always had a raisin under it, but appeared sometimes to the monkey's left, sometimes to his right. It took a little time for the monkey to learn that green was the clue to success. Then Harlow changed the problem, and the monkey had to learn that a triangular lid, wherever it was, concealed the raisin. In the end the monkey needed only one trial to discover which lid covered the prize, even when new shapes or colours were introduced.

Quick results, and carefully rewarding the correct response, are the two chief lessons of operant conditioning research. Practice and repetition, while essential, are not enough. Whether you are a novice pianist or about to tackle an advanced study by Bach; whether you are a newly-wed learning to cook for the first time or a *Cordon Bleu* learning a new-style cuisine, *shaping* is how you learn.

You start by learning the general rules or outline of what you want to do—the basic skill of finger movements, the sequence of notes, the method of combining ingredients or the special use of soyabeans and quick frying. You monitor your progress carefully. If you are a beginner you will probably have a teacher who rewards correct moves with praise. Your teacher should also extinguish false moves by ignoring them or by helping you to distinguish between right and wrong responses. Gradually, as your grasp of the new skill becomes better and you begin to see the next step, you should be able to reinforce yourself by recognising which responses are correct and which are mistaken.

Making your mistakes better

If you find yourself making mistakes when you are learning something new, stop. You are learning to incorporate the mistakes. In these circumstances, practice will make you worse, not better, and your mistakes will become 'perfect'. Start again, but practise very slowly and carefully, so that you do not make mistakes. Speed up again only in stages, keeping fault-free all the time. Whenever you make a mistake, drop a notch or two in speed. Do not try to reach target speed in a single attempt. Take a break and do something else when you are about halfway home. This is so that *satiation* (a condition in which you are satisfied with your progress and will not continue because you have had enough of the effort involved in any learning task) and *inhibition* (suppression or restraint of your behaviour) do not set in and interfere with good learning.

You can, however, use satiation to eliminate mistakes. For example, some concert pianists who play the same pieces many times find that mistakes gradually creep in. Practising correctly is no good to them: they already know the music. So they practise the mistakes over and over again. After a while satiation sets in and the mistakes actually become more difficult to play than the correct version.

Attention, approval, affection...

'Flattery will get you anywhere,' we say flippantly. Yet, almost without realising it, we are talking about the use of three powerful *social reinforcers*—attention, approval and affection. It is the application of operant conditioning to social life.

Attention, approval and affection...

In an experiment some years ago, a college student was observed while engrossed in a supposedly informal conversation with the experimenter. Unbeknown to the student, the experimenter had decided in advance to reinforce all statements of opinion made by the subject, such as sentences beginning 'I think ...' or 'I believe ...'. The reinforcement was the experimenter's saying 'You're right,' 'I agree' and 'That's so'. In another part of the experiment, extinction was carried out by silence following a statement of opinion.[8]

The student's statements of opinion showed a marked increase in frequency when *verbal reinforcement* was carried out. They decreased following extinction. The student remained entirely unaware of the whole process.

Man or machine?

It is easy to latch on to generalisations—to reduce everything to one simple answer. 'It's all sex ...' we tend to say. And, until recently, many behaviourist psychologists believed that learning was 'all conditioning'. They thought that all learning took place through conditioned responses and reinforcement—classical or operant conditioning.

A growing school now accepts that, although conditioning accounts for much of human behaviour, it is not responsible for it all. Think of a small child who has learnt to cross a busy road cautiously by a conditioned set of prohibitions instilled by fear. As the child grows older, it needs to learn for itself a true understanding of the complexities of traffic—that earlier conditioning has to be removed.

Too young to understand the traffic patterns, small children must learn safe road behaviour by rules, sanctioned by punishment and reward.

Thus, although we are mechanical in a large part of our behaviour and learning, this is probably not the only way in which we learn (if it were, we should be reduced to the state of automata or robots). But it is often difficult to say which component—conditioning or reasoned choice—dominates any particular behaviour. For example, take the man who has been conditioned to behave in an obsequious way towards his social superiors. His training may have given him no option but to behave in this manner. On the other hand, he may have come to the realisation that a wider range of behaviour is open to him and decided that pandering to his superiors would be the most productive choice.

A similar thing could be said of tantrum children. Their constant fiery outbursts may be conditioned responses—or calculated devices which they have found to be useful.

The umbrellas represent socially conditioned behaviour: the frogman has exercised a choice.

'Who, me? You've got to be joking.' Even laboratory animals can, and do, make choices about whether they will take their designated parts in experiments.

Take your cue

Rather than responding rigidly to direct stimuli, we seem to be able to use selectivity in our behaviour. Some psychologists are now using the words 'cues' or 'signals' in place of the term 'stimuli'—and these cues that we receive may or may not be acted upon.

This exercising of choice is not confined to mature humans. Even animals have been shown to digress from the 'stimulus–response' path. Two psychologists, Breland and Breland,[9] described a number of 'disobedient' subjects in their animal experiments. There was the chicken who would not sit still, the racoon who refused to put money into a slot, rabbits who balked at approaching the feeder and the stubborn pig who just would not put tokens into a piggy bank . . .

Putting it to the test

B. F. Skinner, who firmly believes that without reinforcement there would be no learning, devised a teaching machine that delivered sweets every time a correct response was made by a child who was being taught. It soon became clear, however, that the child progressed just as quickly with no reward at all. The satisfaction of learning was sufficient reinforcement on its own.

This realisation has been put to practical use by modern educationalists. Teaching machines have been invented not to deliver goodies but to flash lights, play merry jingles or ring bells each time students perform satisfactorily. Immediate feedback of this nature is beneficial to learning. And, predictably, enthusiastic learning is encouraged by prompt knowledge of examination results rather than the customary long delays.

Shaping behaviour

There are three kinds of reinforcement: positive, negative, and punishment. *Positive reinforcement* is the giving of a reward after a wanted response so that it is more likely to occur again. *Negative reinforcement* consists of providing some unpleasant stimulus that is only removed when the wanted response is made. *Punishment* means applying an unpleasant stimulus after a response that is not wanted.

Research with animals has shown that positive reinforcement is overwhelmingly the most effective form of shaping behaviour. Negative reinforcement is unreliable in its effectiveness, and punishment often produces undesired side-effects.

How should punishment be used?

Does this mean that 'spare the rod and spoil the child' is untrue? Some psychologists would say 'yes'. If properly devised programmes of positive reinforcement are followed, it should, theoretically, never be necessary to use punishment in training a child. In practice, of course, only the most fortunate of parents will get by without it. So how, if it is inevitable, should punishment be used?

First, in accordance with basic conditioning principles, there should be good discrimination, so that it is clear exactly what behaviour is being punished. Without this, correct learning cannot take place. Second, punishment should follow as soon after the unwanted behaviour as possible. With children under about three, this means immediately: punishment delivered after a delay at this age will be at best ineffective and may bewilder the

It may relieve the teacher's feelings, but there is little chance that 'a clip on the ear' will modify a child's behaviour patterns.

47

child and make him less amenable to good conditioning later—in other words, rebellious.

Third, there should always be room for the child to manoeuvre. The child should have the opportunity of making a new response that can be rewarded positively. Fourth, punishment should be unambiguous. It should not be mixed, especially, with any expression of triumph or the child will feel that he, not the response, is being punished. Nor should punishment be mixed with positive feelings. In this case the child will receive both punishment and positive reinforcement and he will be confused. Such confusion can lead to the devaluation of either the punishment, or the positive response, or both.

If punishment seems essential, then remember St. Ignatius's advice: 'hate the sin but not the sinner'. Zimbardo and Ruch[10] updated this maxim to read 'punish the response, not the person'. On no account should punishment be linked to general remarks about the child, such as 'You are stupid, wicked, naughty', or 'I suppose I can't expect anything else from you'.

Punishment can become contagious—those who experience it are more likely to go on and punish others. The process is sometimes termed identification with the aggressor. Punishment is also often *context or situation specific* in its effect. Punishing a child for bad behaviour in the home may have no effect on that child's behaviour outside the home. In society at large, or in the family, reliance upon punishment can lead to (or derive from) an authoritarian view that intensive surveillance is vital. The underlying assumption is that a punished person is incapable of managing things for him or herself.

Downgrading the whole person can have few, if any, beneficial results. And this is a danger with another form of discipline often found in 'liberal' middle-class families. Here the negative reinforcement is not a smack or a cross word but the withdrawal of affection. At first sight this may appear to be a more humane method of instilling good behaviour. However, there is a real danger that the child will come to devalue himself. Feeling worthless is the first step on the road to general rebelliousness. And withdrawal of affection can also produce a general inability to give self-reinforcement. As with more overt forms of punishment the danger here is that the practice is self-justifying. A naughty child is punished, the punishment is ineffective and so the child is punished yet again—and so on.

Conditioning self-control

In this final part of the chapter, let us look at how principles of conditioning relate to bodily functions which until recently were thought to be beyond the pale of conditioning. Psychologist Neal Miller, an influential figure in the field of learning theory, suggested that the differences between classical and operant conditioning were more apparent than real.[11] He and his associates showed quite dramatically how automatic responses could be conditioned by both operant and classical processes. Laboratory rats were taught to control blood pressure, heart rate, intestinal contractions and even urine formation. In some amazing experiments, rats were actually conditioned to send blood to one ear and not the other.

Miller's work opened up the floodgates for the investigation of *biofeedback* processes (see Chapter 2). It is still too early for the practical implications of this ability to have taken root in mainstream therapeutic services. But research carries with it the promise of a greater understanding of such phenomena as altered states of consciousness, self-awareness and self-control.

Biofeedback techniques have much to gain from the East, especially from those cultures emphasising the importance of meditation, which has long claimed control over autonomic bodily functions. Years of learning and dedication have enabled Yogis and Zen masters to control their brainwaves, heartbeat and body temperature. Western scientists experimenting with these skills have learnt much from the daily practices of Zen buddhists, for example.

It was reasonably assumed that Zen priests should, during periods of meditation, display the physiological concomitants of attentiveness and awareness. In psychophysiological terms these are reflected by a high frequency of alpha brainwaves (attentiveness) and continual responsiveness to incoming stimuli (awareness). Both these assumptions are confirmed in an experiment by biofeedback researchers. The Zen priests showed high frequency of alpha brainwaves and uniformly responded to each fresh presentation of a particular stimulus in exactly the same way as they did to the first presentation. (Were they perhaps sensing the world anew at each new sign of life?)

Pavlov's dogs, absentee workers and spoilt children may seem an oddball list, but in this chapter we have seen how they are related through the basic principles of classical and operant conditioning. We have also seen that conditioning can occur without any conscious effort on our own part. The common thread running through all approaches to learning is the search for understanding; for meaning, for ways of making sense. We search for patterns, keys, codes which simplify learning. We learn new things and link them with the old we already know. We look for logic and order in making sense of the learning processes. We are actually learning how to interpret our whole world.

An integral part of this process is our capacity to store all that we experience, ready to be retrieved when needed. Learning engages the brain in different activities that probably leave persisting physical traces of themselves—retrievable information. This information is 'stored' in memory. How this happens—and how we can make memory work more efficiently—is what the next chapter is all about.

4 Remembering and forgetting

During the hot summer of 1976, a young relative of mine was knocked unconscious in his school yard. Although 'out' for only a couple of minutes, he was quite disoriented when he came round. For several hours he couldn't remember what day it was even though he was repeatedly told—'Wednesday.' And for five hours he had no recollection of what had happened to cause his state of confusion and anxiety. Gradually, however, he reconstructed the events leading up to his short spell of unconsciousness. The names of his friends came back first, then the sequence in a game of playground football. He was standing close to the ball and, seeing his chance to break through, he ran on to the ball; unfortunately the boot of an opposition player caught the young boy's head as he moved in. That was that.

Inventing the past

This true story illustrates some important facts about memory. First, a blow to the head can cause memory failure. Those who lose consciousness in automobile accidents often find that they are unable to recall how the accident happened. The accident seems to have destroyed their consciousness of the experience *before it has had time to take root in the memory.* Events leading up to the crash—stopping for coffee, say, even 15 minutes before the impact—are often lost as well. In other words, a blow seems to 'shake free' some material that has already been stored in the memory.

Accidents are all too frequent in modern society and the temporary loss of memory which sometimes follows them is common knowledge. But the story of the young boy playing football reveals a far more important aspect of how we remember. Because he was *not* knocked out by a football boot, as his friends were aware. The game of football he remembered had taken place a whole week earlier. On the Wednesday of his accident he was playing with the same friends, in the same playground when, during a rough and tumble chasing game, he fell and struck his head on the sunbaked earth. What the boy had done was to 'remember' a sequence of events that explained his present

Still a long way to go.

condition. The memory, that is the story he *constructed*, was quite in line with the boy's interests and habits—but totally incorrect. His memory had taken various pieces of information and produced a reasonable, meaningful narrative.

More complex than computers

Until quite recently, psychologists assumed that the human memory worked like a computer, or a card index system: put information in, get the same information back (even if the process of retrieval was sometimes messy and some cards were inexplicably lost). We now know that the mechanism of human memory is far more complex than that of the most advanced computer. When we remember something we *reconstruct* in a creative way: adding bits here, cutting bits there, shaping and moulding in order to produce a *meaningful* pattern.

If a blow to the head causes loss of memory, the brain will attempt to compensate by using available bits of information and suggesting probable and coherent scenarios. Sometimes, like the boy in the playground, we accept such a suggestion—we 'remember' something that never happened.

For most of us, for most of the time, memory is an unquestioned facility. It works well enough. Occasionally we are surprised by some unsolicited recollection. Too often we are embarrassed by our inability to put a name to a face. But how often do we stop to think about this amazing ability we have to remember things?

'Do you remember when . . .?' But we are not simply recorders: we create our pasts, and they may not always match reality.

Too little—and too much

Life would be terrifying without memory. We would exist in a whirlwind of frightening 'firsts'. Certain victims of brain damage, for example, are known to live in such a horrific, continuously and instantaneously renewed world. Without memory there would be no speech, no social relationships, no art, politics or football games. It is not too much to say that if the human race lacked memory it simply would not be.

At the other extreme, memory can be too perfect. The Russian neuro-physiologist, Luria, has detailed the case of 'S', a man with total and almost uncontrollable recall.[1] There was little rhyme or reason to his recollection. Important events would be chased away by detailed recollections of the most trivial occasions. And while most of us concentrate on remembering, 'S' had to produce techniques of forgetting.

As time went by, he found it increasingly difficult to cope with reality. Just as a person without memory can only exist at the precise instant, 'S' became unable to recognise 'now'. Perception and memory fused together; immediate experience and images of the past jostled for his attention and caused extreme confusion.

Memory at work

We should be grateful for our reasonably efficient middle-of-the-road memories. But how does memory work? Can we improve its efficiency?

Memory is a system with three sequences: input, storage and retrieval. In order to remember something, we must first have experienced it (disregarding exceptional cases like the boy who banged his head): this is input. We must also have stored it and, of course, we must be able to retrieve it from the memory store. But the system is far more complicated than that schematic account indicates. Memory is a dynamic process involving creative organisation and reconstruction. And although a severe blow to the head can 'shake out' some of our memories, those who search for some secret 'box' to hold them in the brain have little success. Karl Lashley, a psychologist of great rigour and ingenuity, spent a lifetime trying to locate the seat of memory. Systematically slicing into the brains of trained rats, he found that vast volumes of grey matter had to be surgically removed before what the rat had learned became lost.[2]

The results obtained by another researcher are even more intriguing. Pietsch conducted several hundred operations on salamanders. His plan was not to remove parts of the brain, but to *reorganise* it. He showed that complex shuffling of the brain had little or no effect upon the salamander's memory. So how is information stored? How can it be that areas of brain can be juggled or removed without affecting memory, while a crack on the head can erase a dramatic event in someone's life?

The hologram analogy

One possible explanation is given by an analogy with discoveries in modern physics. Dennis Gabor, a physicist at the University of London, is credited with discovering an amazing form of photography. He found that if a photographic plate, without lenses, was exposed to an object illuminated by laser beams, a most peculiar process took place. The plate itself took on a complex pattern of whirls and dots. But if he then shone laser light through this plate the original object appeared to be recreated *in three dimensions*. Such 'holograms' have a ghostly appearance. They are solid images that float in the air; they can be walked round and walked through. Nor is that all: an exposed hologram plate can be shattered into the smallest of pieces, but each piece, when illuminated correctly, will recreate the original image.

Many psychologists argue that this principle of storage—and it is still barely understood—could apply to memory. To be more exact, they believe that memory is not located in some corner of the brain, but is a function of the *overall pattern of brain activity*. If this is the case, then, as with the holographic plate, the brain can be shuffled (Pietsch) or reduced in size (Lashley) without necessarily destroying stored information. This is an important theory because it emphasises patterns and processes, which links with findings that show that the memory is not a mechanical device but a system of organisation which strives for meaningful patterns.

Memory seems to have three levels. First there is a brief, exact and brilliant 'sensory storage' system which is almost akin to consciousness itself. Sensory storage (which lasts for less than a second) allows immediate 'action replay' without any loss of detail. From this level information goes directly to a 'short-term' memory store where it lives on for a further twenty seconds or so. Deliberate effort is required to transfer short-term entries to the third stage of the process, the long-term memory system. We organise or repeat shopping lists or directions. Without that effort they are lost. Memory can be improved by concentrating on this stage of transfer from short term to long term.

Having a memory means we are only amazed once by something outside our experience . . .

The sum of our experiences is stored in the long-term memory systems. Evidence suggests that, with training, or while under

hypnosis, huge portions of life can be retrieved from the long-term stores. Arranged in some mysterious, maybe 'holographic', way and contained within each individual's brain is a unique and all-embracing autobiography.

Why do we forget?

If we did not forget, we should be reduced to the state of confusion experienced by Luria's acquaintance, S. In a sense, forgetting is essential to survival. But why is it that when we actually want to remember something we cannot always bring it to mind?

Several factors are involved, but the list is less straightforward than you might imagine. 'It all happened so long ago . . .' we say. And yet there is no scientific evidence that time itself causes forgetting. Learned skills such as cycling, driving and swimming

. . . and once we have adapted ourselves to it, we never forget how to handle it.

quickly return after long periods of neglect. We can all recall events from childhood—indeed the aged often report clearer recall of childhood than of more recent events. Those in solitary confinement—there are enough ex-hostages and ex-prisoners around the world for us to have significant information on this—often dredge their memories, turning up countless past experiences and pieces of verse or prose learned many years earlier. Contrary to popular belief, time itself doesn't seem to wipe out our past experiences.

But time is indirectly implicated in forgetting. During quite short periods of time, events can occur that *interfere* with the establishment of information in the memory stores. Surprisingly perhaps, learning something similar to the information to be recalled is most disruptive. You can try this simple experiment to demonstrate this effect.

Copy out the twelve 'nonsense' syllables shown in *List 1* and get a friend to do likewise. Both of you should spend five minutes learning the syllables in *List 1*. Now ask your friend to relax for five minutes while you try to memorise *List 2*. Finally, on separate sheets of paper, both try to write out the syllables from *List 1*.

You will almost certainly find that your friend does much better than you. By learning *List 2*, you have interfered with the establishment of *List 1* in your memory. Your friend did not have this problem. *List 2* acts backwards, as it were, and influences how well you can remember *List 1*, a process known as *retroactive inhibition*.

But interference, or inhibition, can also work forwards (as well as backwards). Such interference is called *proactive inhibition*. Learn *List 3*. Then, as in the first experiment, get a friend to join you in learning *List 4*. Now, as before, both of you attempt to recreate *List 4* on separate pieces of paper. Again you lose. Learning *List 3* has interfered with your learning of the last list—proactive inhibition is at work.

List 1

| FOF, | DUT, | LEB, | PID, | HAF, | ROP, |
| SUW, | BOC, | RIS, | BAF, | GIR, | HAB. |

List 2

| CIR, | DAC, | GIZ, | WAB, | POG, | RUZ, |
| HES, | JUQ, | KIW, | QON, | MIB, | LUW. |

List 3

| POR, | GAR, | NOL, | GAC, | LUN, | BEC, |
| KEB, | BIV, | TUL, | FID, | KAC, | PES. |

List 4

| LUB, | MOJ, | RIJ, | KIB, | HUJ, | JUP, |
| PAG, | QUD, | WUF, | GAJ, | CEV, | DOB. |

Meaningful reminders

Nonsense syllables like the ones you have just been working with have been used in psychology experiments for a hundred years. They have the advantage of being more or less meaningless. If you had used words related to your occupation, several other factors would have been at work in the simple experiment you have just conducted. Or let us say that your friend is French-Canadian while you have no knowledge of the French language. Would it have been a fair test to use a dozen common French words?

But even nonsense syllables carry some sort of meaning or familiarity. You will find that a list of words such as ZOP, POB, ING, HAN, is much easier to remember than, say, UOY, KFI, PWK. Memory works on meaningfulness, and pronounceability, and the first syllables *sound* more meaningful—because they represent sequences of letters occurring in most European languages—than the second, even if both sets mean exactly nothing.

Another reason why our memories can give faulty results has already been mentioned in the story of the boy who was knocked out. His memory *created* a recollection that wasn't accurate. Skilled interviewers are aware that we often 'remember' inferences from material that we have been given. Lawyers are particularly sensitive to this feature of memory when they are cross-examining a witness. 'Did you see anyone attack the old lady?' can elicit a quite different recollection from the one induced by 'Did you see a man attack the old lady?'

An experiment proves the point. Students were shown a short film of two cars in collision and then asked to estimate the speed of the cars. One group was asked: 'About how fast were the two cars going when they smashed into each other?' The other group was asked, 'How fast were the cars going when they bumped into each other?' Remember that both groups saw the same film. Could the different words—'smashed' and 'bumped'—affect their memory of the speed? The answer is 'yes'—and the effect was dramatic. The first group (smashed) gave an average estimate of 40 mph, the second group (bumped) suggested 30 mph.

Breakdowns

Meaningfulness and organisation are clearly indicated in abnormal breakdowns such as amnesia and fugue. The *fugue*—a period of time during which the sufferer may move off to a new town and behave in uncharacteristic ways—is a strange case of memory dysfunction. When the victim of fugue 'comes round' all the events that occurred during the sometimes lengthy attack are lost. The fugue and the events that occur during it seem to be related to extremely complex processes of inhibition and anxiety. Victims are given a new life for a short time—and no responsibility for their actions. Amnesia, a less specific loss of memory, may result from brain damage, but it also seems that some cases of amnesia arise as a consequence of the represssion of memories.

Repression, in which the memory is 'locked' away, need not be seriously incapacitating. Quite extreme cases of amnesia have been reported in which the sufferer has maintained an apparently ordinary workaday life. Sigmund Freud argued that all forgetting (along with unplanned puns and slips of the tongue) is in fact motivated. We forget many things that would be embarrassing or injurious to us. We 'repress' episodes from childhood that might cause us to experience anxiety or guilt.

Although Freud's theory is not susceptible to scientific corroboration and is less all-embracing than has been suggested, it has a ring of truth, a certain pragmatic rightness most of us will recognise. Anxiety *can* be involved in quite simple failures to remember. Consider the elusive name that slips from your mind just as you need it. It's there on the tip of your tongue. But the harder you try, the more desperate you feel. And the less likely you are to remember it.

If you cannot remember it, stop worrying. As your anxiety decreases, the name will probably float into your consciousness.

Don't cloud the issues

Memory, therefore, is clearly influenced by the character of the information to be remembered, our state of mind and various other factors. The situation in which we memorise information is also important. The concepts of retroactive and proactive inhibition make it clear that learning should be conducted at a steady pace. If you need to know something in the morning, learn it before sleeping. And don't 'cloud the issue' with unnecessary facts. Endel Tulving, a psychologist from the University of Toronto, has explored factors that help and hinder remembering when the person has only a few seconds in which to absorb lists of words.[3] His results are fascinating, not least because of their complexity.

Some people can recall words presented in this way if they are asked to remember them in the room where they were learned. Others do better if they are given 'cues' which are unrelated to the lists, and so on. Tulving argues that remembering is a constructive process which depends upon the 'memory traces' themselves *and* the 'cognitive environment' of the rememberer at the time of retrieval. Memory is related to one's 'general state of mind', emphasising once again the importance of organisation and meaningfulness.

Year by year, as specialists conduct sophisticated researches, memory is emerging as one of the most amazing of all human faculties. We cannot really expect easy explanations for an ability that locates us in time and records our own individuality, and on which in real terms our sensation of 'life' depends.

Although a final explanation of the physiology of memory has yet to be arrived at, humans have since the beginnings of history had enough understanding of its workings in practice to devise ways of making it more efficient. The rules are few—avoid anxiety; organise the material to be memorised.

Put simply, anxiety is the enemy of memory, relaxation its

friend. If you are keyed-up, feeling tense, take a few minutes off before attempting to memorise important facts. And then organise them. By organising facts before they 'go in' you are increasing the efficiency of your memory stores—you will remember them better. Do not try to memorise things you don't understand. Take the time to understand and organise.

Ways of improving memory

Try some memory tricks, as useful now as when the ancient Greek orators used them. There are many variations on three basic mnemonic strategies: context and imagery, visualisation, and mnemonic sentences. All improve with use and are based upon association—which is another way of saying organisation.

Reminder: some people might have contented themselves with knotting a handkerchief!

Context and imagery   Memory can be increased as much as seven-fold by the use of an appropriate *context*. Take a shopping list as an example. You need, say, shoes, matches, pears, cauliflower, an electric plug, raisins and a belt. Weave these unrelated items into a simple story—to relate them within a context. The more outrageous the puns and jokes the better— you'll have little difficulty in remembering them! Here's an example for the above shopping list. 'I need *shoes*, a *pair* that *matches* the colour of *cauliflowers*. I'm *raisin* my hopes, *plugging* away at the *shoe* shops. Just look at the time.... I must *belt* on home.'

This is one of the few techniques where the most bizarre strategies or stories often turn out best.

Visual imagery   is another useful technique. Imagine a room you know well, or a garden—even a map or a doll's house will do. Having got that firmly established, just 'hide' your facts about the room. When you need to recall them, re-establish the room in your mind and hunt around. The facts will all be there.

Mnemonic schemes: using visual imagery. 'Your face is familiar, but I can't recall your mane ...!' Visualisation would help to remember Mr Leo Ridout.

Acronymics   A mnemonic strategy often used by psychology students who wish to remember one of the ways of classifying various psychoneuroses is: AH! MAD COP. The initial letters act as the pegs on which to hang the neuroses: *A*nxiety, *H*ypochondria, *M*ultiple personality, *A*mnesia, *D*epressive neurosis, *C*onversion hysteria, *O*bsessional compulsions and *P*hobias.

For almost all lists that have to be learned by students there exist time-honoured sentences, many of which are too vulgar for the printed page. Making up your own mnemonic sentences is a fun activity which increases the efficiency of a truly remarkable facility of the human brain.

Here are a few more guidelines to learning more efficiently.
Whole or part? Is it simpler to learn a 12-line poem as a 'poem-of-12-lines', or as 12 separate lines? Here, the whole method is better than the part method. But this does not always hold true, as tennis players will testify. Learning individual strokes and tactical manoeuvres improves the quality of the whole game.

Learning to swim is best learned as a whole.

Massed or distributed practice Learn a little at a time rather than trying it on all at once. If you can devote two hours a day to learning something—divide the time into half-hourly stints. Apparently the brain needs time to consolidate input and permanently record it in the long-term memory bank. Study before sleep seems also to be a useful dictum.

Feedback Monitoring your performance as you learn enables you to pick out any problems as and when they occur. It makes learning more exciting, too: expectation and curiosity are important factors in stimulating the process.

Not just a record bin

Two related themes have been emphasised throughout this chapter: organisation and meaning. The memory is not a simple storage system for unrelated facts and experiences: it is a dynamic process which operates most effectively on meaningful, well-organised material.

In the last two chapters we have seen that our ability to learn, our susceptibility to operant and classical conditioning, and our memories, enable us to cope with life. These faculties allow us to live fruitful and satisfying lives. What makes us decide exactly *what* will be fruitful and satisfying and drives us on to attain it? Chapter 5 discusses human motivation.

5 Looking for a motive

Some people believe that all human behaviour is motivated by an essential selfishness. They regard even altruism as simply a devious means of 'getting your own way'. Others believe in the 'goodness' and selflessness of humanity. Most of us, sensibly, take a position somewhere between these two extremes, realising that motivation varies from one situation to the next for the majority of people. But such views are not explanations *of human behaviour in any scientific sense. They are viewpoints or articles of faith, themselves open to retrospective explanation but giving few clues as to how a particular person* will *behave in a given situation. A scientific description must be such that it will allow you to predict what will happen in given circumstances and to be sure that in those particular circumstances the same thing will always happen.*

Are we governed by instincts?

One of the earliest attempts to explain motivation was known as the *instinct theory*, and was popular in the early 1900s. According to this theory, developed by William McDougall, each person has separate instincts for such things as escape, combat, self-assertion, self-abasement, and all the other elements that go to make up human behaviour. But instincts fail to explain the dynamics of behaviour, merely reducing it to a prodigious list of convenient labels. Anthropologists also discovered that supposedly universal 'instincts' such as jealousy, rivalry, maternity and self-defence were weak or non-existent in societies that placed no emphasis on them. The theory has long been discarded: nevertheless the word 'instinct' remains in common use. We often say 'I acted on instinct' or 'my instinct tells me . . .' when we mean to describe motives so deeply embedded that we are not conscious of them or 'cannot help' them.

Some schools of psychological thought would go to the opposite extreme from McDougall's theory of instincts, and deny that such a thing as motivation—as it is commonly understood—exists at all. The behaviourists, for example, believe that motives are simply not necessary to explain behaviour. All

Does the child need to beg? Can the man afford to give? This is South Africa, and motives— the driving force of behaviour—reflect stereotyped expectations of who plays which role.

of human behaviour, they say, no matter how complex, can be described in terms of hierarchies of conditioned responses and learned activities. They also point to the very basis of scientific explanation—the notion of cause and effect. Events do not just occur, they are caused. And causes *always precede effects*. But motives are expressed in terms of goals: 'I did this because I wanted that.' In other words, 'my behaviour was shaped by something that hadn't yet happened.' That is no kind of explanation to offer to a hard-line behaviourist.

Drives for survival

In the present state of the world's population, contraception may reflect the drive for survival better than reproduction.

What the behaviourist will accept is that the mainsprings of behaviour are to be found in certain *primary drives* essential to personal survival and the survival of the species. They argue that the manipulation of these drives—intake of food, liquid and oxygen, along with sexual behaviour—can lead to total control over the individual. Without these prerequisites, neither the individual nor the species can survive. These are known as primary drives because they are *unlearned* sources of energy—and therefore survival—in an organism or species.

Hunger, as one of these primary drives, has been the subject of much animal experimentation. Scientists have made countless attempts to analyse hunger and eating. Yet even experiments conducted on blowflies—often considered to be little more than living machines—have shown that the process is by no means simple. What then of the higher animals, and ourselves?

Our appetites are highly differentiated. In order to maintain the human body in good working order we need balanced amounts of protein, carbohydrates, iron, numerous vitamins and other elements. A 'healthy' diet contains enough of these requirements to meet our needs. When the diet falls short of a vital substance, or some defect causes an increased need for a certain vitamin or trace element, it may be experienced as a 'sub-hunger': our search for food will be directed accordingly.

Self-service meals

In a famous experiment, C. M. Davis let three newly-weaned infants eat whatever they liked at every meal.[1] Apart from occasional binges, the children followed a balanced overall diet. One child, who started the experiment with rickets (caused by vitamin D deficiency), cured himself by consuming extra cod liver oil.

The diet offered to these children consisted only of 'real' food. 'Junk' foods, like ice cream, cola drinks and so on, or unusually rich foods such as cream cakes, were not included. This is an important aspect of the study because other experiments suggest that taste is a very powerful factor in shaping diet. Rats in the laboratory will reject a nutritious liquid that has been made bitter with quinine in favour of a saccharine solution of no food value.

The validity of such experiments depends, indeed, on not confusing the issues in this way. And that the experimental requirements are valid is well illustrated by the experience of Britain during and after the Second World War. Rickets decreased dramatically during the war because government rationing policy ensured balanced 'real' diets with very little 'junk'. But 30 years after the end of the war, rickets had re-appeared: when they were free to choose among a surplus of foods, some sectors of the population were wooed away from a balanced diet to a large consumption of 'sweets' or candies, related primarily to people's desire for pleasure but also to the skilled commercial exploitation of these profitable 'goodies'.

The principle that you will eat what is good for you works, therefore, only in conditions of restricted food supply. When food is in surplus, animals—and humans—do not seem to behave quite as sensibly. Overeating in response to hunger cues has in fact become a serious 'disease'.

Fat, fatter, fatal!

Obesity can have fatal results, and not many people actually like to be fat. Why, then, do some people overeat and get fat? What motivates them? There are many theories, and the causes of

'Inside every fat man a thin man is trying to get out'—but what keeps him in may be a more intricate psychological lock than mere gluttony.

obesity are undoubtedly various and complex. But one promising line of research, into the physical and eating habits of obese and normal-weight individuals, provides some interesting clues to motivation in general as well as casting light on the way, if not the only reason why, people get fat.

First, the internal messages for hunger (such as stomach contractions) differ significantly between the two groups. Fatter people seem to feel contractions more often than they actually occur, and this, in part, stimulates them to eat more often. And when fat people do eat, they eat as much on a full stomach as they do on an empty one. Moreover, emotions such as fear, tension, anxiety, do not decrease their appetite for food.

'Time span' is another important motivator. Most of us have been conditioned to feel hungry every four to six hours during the day. For the obese amongst us, this programme is intensely difficult to maintain because the mere *thought* that it is time to eat makes them hungry.

Dinner time happens because that is when we feel hungry—unless we are chronically fat, when we may feel hungry simply because it is dinner time!

Nisbett and Schachter have demonstrated the power of external cues on 'motivation to eat'.[2] In a laboratory study they examined obese and normal-weight individuals under 'deceptive' conditions. They rigged the wall clocks in the windowless experiment rooms, so that they could be speeded up, or slowed down. One set of clocks were set to run at about twice normal speed, whilst others were cut down to about half speed.

Participants were led to believe that they were taking part in a study measuring physiological parameters. Consequently, they had electrodes attached to their wrists, thus giving the experimenters a legitimate excuse to remove watches. The experiments began at 5 p.m. and were scheduled to last for thirty minutes. At 5.30 p.m. the experimenters entered the rooms eating from a box of biscuits. Slow clocks showed 5.20 p.m. Fast clocks showed 6.05 p.m. The experimenter would place his box of biscuits on the table, inviting the participant to help himself, and then would leave the room having requested the subject to fill in a questionnaire. The box of biscuits remained in the room.

Obese subjects who thought it was 6.05 p.m. (closer to dinner time), ate *twice* as much as those who thought it was 5.20 p.m.! Normal-weight subjects ate *less* when they thought it was closer to dinner time (presumably not wanting to spoil their appetites) than otherwise.

If, however, fat people have to 'work' for their food—especially when the effort involved is annoying or frustrating—they do not eat as much as they would otherwise do. For example, overweight people in the habit of eating pre-shelled peanuts will eat significantly less if they have to shell the peanuts themselves.

Those of normal weight show no difference in peanut consumption, pre-shelled or otherwise.

'Eating means comfort'

Why is it that fat people are unable to withstand the powerful impact of the external cues in the environment? One theory follows the maxim: 'A fat baby makes a fat child makes a fat adult'.

A newborn baby cries when it is hungry. But not all mothers realise that infants also cry when they are uncomfortable, wet, in pain, angry, frustrated or lonely. The non-discriminating mother tends to feed her child every time it cries. The infant thus fails to differentiate between hunger and the various other arousal states which cause its anguish.

The child grows up learning that *all* internal 'deprivation' stimuli signal hunger. Such children will therefore eat every time they are negatively aroused. Alternatively, unlike normal-weight individuals who rely predominantly on internal hunger cues, the growing fat child may be unable to recognise internal hunger cues at all. These children then come to rely solely on external cues in the environment for the guidance and direction of their eating habits. This explanation dispenses entirely with 'motive' if that word is interpreted as the pursuit of a goal.

First things first

But can you really explain your friends' or your own behaviour solely in terms of learning? Is all behaviour closely tied to survival? Consider vanity, jealousy, love, ambition, the search for joy and personal fulfilment—the strongest 'motives', as we think of them. There are those who argue that the behaviourists' understanding is too limited to encompass the richness of human experience. For example behaviourists may find difficulty in explaining inter-specific altruism. (The classic example of Greyfriars Bobby, an Edinburgh dog, comes to mind; he pined to death at his master's grave.) And even more would agree that, since people understand and use the concept of motivation, the concept must be a legitimate part of a science of people. In order to understand a person we must understand how he understands himself. One psychologist who devoted considerable time to developing this so-called *humanist* approach to psychology is Abraham Maslow.

Maslow proposed that we have a *hierarchy of needs*.[3] The most elementary are the biological needs of hunger, thirst, sleep and so forth, and these come first. Higher needs cannot normally be met until the elementary needs are taken care of. Safety and bodily comfort come next: a castaway on a desert island will seek food before he starts to build a shelter; and when hunger pangs return he will abandon building work.

Above these needs comes love, which includes, in Maslow's eyes, affection as well as sex. This is Maslow's first major difference from the behaviourist theories. To the pure behaviourist, affection is a learned response to another person. It is

Pairing off: learned behaviour or an inbuilt drive?

reinforced by reduction of the sex or hunger drives. And it is elaborated and maintained by learned secondary drives and reinforcement systems.

Our need for affection is a bridge between the lower biological needs and the higher psychological needs. Immediately above affection comes self-esteem, and the good regard of others. A man who is able to earn enough to keep himself fed and housed seeks out a mate and probably starts a family. When these needs are met, he starts to worry about what his work-mates think of him and whether his job meets the standard he would like to set himself.

Finally, Maslow refers to a need for self-development and liberation, which he terms *self-actualisation*. Neither self-esteem nor self-actualisation has any place in the theoretical arsenal of the behaviourists.

Maslow argues that these needs operate in two ways at once. Or rather, that the lowest two operate in one way, as *deficiency* needs, whilst the top two are *growth* needs. Affection can be both a growth and a deficiency need. Growth needs are exactly like the body's needs for vitamin C or iodine. We cannot survive without them, and if our diet falls short, we become motivated to seek them out. Maslow places great emphasis on affection, both given and received. According to him, *all* neuroses are caused by a deficiency in affection. This in turn brings about a deficiency in the higher needs.

The 'humanist' school of psychology claims the giving and receiving of affection is a basic human need.

Motivation at work

What motivates people to work this hard? In this case obviously not immediate material reward.

Maslow has become chiefly associated with the humanistic revolution. This emphasises psychological growth rather than the ceaseless striving for material possessions. Paradoxically, it is in industry that his greatest influence may be felt. Industry has long desired to know what motivates a person to work hard, and

very often has settled on payment on some form of 'piece rate', whereby a person is paid in direct proportion to his or her output, as the strongest reason for increasing output.

Frederick Taylor, known as 'Speedy Taylor', invented time and motion studies and showed how increased individual efficiency could improve individual earnings among workers.[4] Yet later in his life he was to write sadly: 'It's a horrid life for any man to live not being able to look any workman in the face without seeing hostility there, and a feeling that every man around you is your virtual enemy.' 'Scientific Management'—the term applied to Taylor's approach—failed because it was based upon too simple a model of the individual.

Rest periods from work may be important in motivation—but having an interest taken in you may be more important still.

Another famous experiment later showed that money and physical working conditions were not the only factors influencing work motivation. At the Hawthorne electrical works Elton Mayo introduced carefully controlled changes in the conditions under which relays were assembled.[5] At the outset, working a 48-hour week with no rest periods, the employees were each producing 2,400 relays a week. First, Mayo introduced piece-work and output went up, as expected. Then, two five-minute rest periods were introduced. Once again output went up. When the rest periods were lengthened to ten minutes output again went up. The company introduced a free hot meal and output rose once more. Finally, the girls were let out at 4.30 instead of 5.00, and output went up still further. Absenteeism declined by 80 per cent during the experiment.

A human interest story

To end the experiment, Mayo made a comparison check when girls went back to their original hard conditions. No one was more surprised than Mayo when production broke all records at over 3,000 relays a week! This phenomenon became known as the 'Hawthorne Effect' and was explained by the fact that the workers responded positively to the *interest that was shown in them*. The whole question of interest may well be extremely important in almost *all* motivation analysis. It could boil down to the desire to make one's life interesting to oneself: not necessarily pleasurable.

Frederick Herzberg believes that people at work are motivated in two ways.[6] The first, the avoidance of pain from the environment, he calls 'Animal-Adam' motivation. The other, which is seeking growth from tasks, he calls 'Human-Abraham' motivation. Herzberg argues that a company cannot prosper unless it meets both kinds of need in its employees.

Another approach to motivation—in this case in managers— has been suggested by David McClelland.[7] He analysed the psychological motivations behind the ways we live and work and found three chief needs: for power, for achievement and for affiliation or fellowship. McClelland found that managers with high need for affiliation tend to dislike the psychological distance of power and are likely to forgo production targets. A manager with a high need for personal power matched by equally high achievement needs may be very effective. He will build a close-knit, highly effective team. But disruption can result if the manager leaves the company, as his 'team' has become far too dependent on the one man.

The best kind of manager a company can employ, in McClelland's view, is one with a high achievement need who invests his power needs in the company. This may be good for the company—but not necessarily in the long-term interests of the manager himself. He is prone to abnormally high rates of hypertension and heart disease. Maslow's theory predicts such an outcome for those who neglect the fulfilment of their needs.

In a revealing application of McClelland's theory, David Winter analysed the patterns of motivation of the front runners of the 1970 American Presidential election (see Table, opposite).[8] He compared these candidates with front runners of earlier years. The contrast between the two final candidates could not have been clearer. Ford carried a reputation as being a 'nice guy—but weak'. And that is what his scores showed. Carter came out with a well-balanced profile showing emphasis on achievement. Humphrey was another 'nice guy', but with a lower power need. Reagan and Wallace both scored high on power and shared a conspicuously low affiliation need.

The remarkable profile of John F. Kennedy may help to explain his unique charisma. He scored high—almost the highest of all—on all three dimensions, need for power, need for affiliation, need for achievement.

	Power	Achievement	Affiliation
Jimmy Carter	50	57	51
Gerald Ford	24	68	63
Hubert Humphrey	44	56	55
Ronald Reagan	53	56	38
George Wallace	59	37	38
John Kennedy	64	60	66
Richard Nixon	49	67	66
Lyndon Johnson	57	63	46
Dwight Eisenhower	44	44	61
Harry Truman	59	49	56
Franklin Roosevelt	55	53	40

Average 50

Achievement and foresight

Perhaps the most interesting—and not the least potent—of these psychological motivators of behaviour is *achievement*. This is a socially-based motive. Achievement motivation enables us to accomplish something important—something of value which will meet our own standards of excellence. We reward and punish each other according to social expectations. We also reward and punish ourselves. In the interests of achievement, we therefore forgo immediate pleasures for the sake of future goals.

This commitment is made not because delay of gratification is a necessary condition of life in today's world. Our capacity for foresight makes it possible. This trait is distinctly human—and perhaps one of the better sides of 'human nature'. Some of our forefathers planted trees for our benefit; our parents save their money for our welfare. We, too, will toil away, through an uncertain future, for others to benefit well beyond the end of our days.

6 Revealing our feelings

Babies gurgle when they are tossed in the air. Children laugh at circus clowns and peculiar noises. We laugh when we are tickled and we laugh when we do the tickling. Jokes, the comedians who tell them and the television programmes which feature them all provoke mirth. We laugh at people's absurdities, when we meet each other after long absences; we laugh when we're in love, drunk, happy, nervous or shy. We even laugh when we're sad. Laughter is just one of many manifestations of emotion that distinguishes the human race from other species: apparently animals never laugh.

Emotions 'light up' our felt state, add colour to plain behaviour and plain statement. We suffer 'black moods', 'get the blues', 'feel in the pink'. A 'deadpan' expression is very likely to invoke the enquiry, 'What's wrong?' If dead or flattened emotion is displayed continuously by a person, he or she may well come to be regarded as psychologically disordered.

Emotion, like motivation, is difficult to define. It is a subjective psychological state often regarded as the overt expression of motivation. When we profess to feel 'emotional', what we mean is that something inside us is 'stirred up' and disturbing. This feeling is usually caused by environmental stimuli, mediated by cognitive or physiological variables.

Fear, rage, hatred, jealousy, ecstasy, are intense emotions. The greater their intensity, the more these feelings disrupt our normal patterns of behaviour. Inadequate handling of emotional reactions has been known to lead to mental disorder and psychosomatic illness.

On the other hand, positive emotions such as love, affection and tenderness promote constructive and satisfying relationships and make life worthwhile.

Charles Darwin suggested that some patterns of emotional expression are innate in animals and humans. But the meanings of these expressions vary from culture to culture—and even from situation to situation. Tears can signify grief or joy; we weep in sorrow, 'cry' with laughter.

Reading emotions

In Western societies, we tend to use silent or *non-verbal communication* to express much of what we want to say. But our signals are not always easy to read. 'Uncomplicated' emotions

Football feelings:
can you spot
supporters of
the team
that hasn't
scored a touchdown?

73

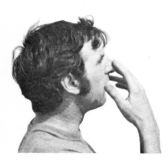

such as surprise, happiness, sadness or anger are easily identified by most people and as we grow older, so identification becomes easier. When more complex emotions such as embarrassment or bewilderment emerge, we rely heavily on *contextual cues* for their identification. Tears at a wedding, at a funeral, or at funny show, gain their meaning, their expressive value, from the context.

In 'reading' other people's emotions we rely on obvious outer clues such as facial expression and body movements. But in the case of our own emotions the hidden aspect is available to us. Do we know exactly how to classify our emotions?

That 'churned up' feeling we get is commonly attributed to bodily changes associated with strong emotions. 'I'm afraid: my heart is pounding', or 'I'm apprehensive—I have butterflies in my stomach'. This apparently commonsense point of view was challenged by two scientists, James and Lange, in the 1880s. They argued that the emotion we experience is the *result* of bodily changes, not the cause of it.

Can you tell from their expressions what emotions these men are experiencing? Check your guesses on page 76 for the one above, page 78 for the one below.

According to James and Lange, a charging bull produces a 'stirred up' internal state, *followed* by fear. When we see the bull, we start running, and then *because* we are running, we begin to feel afraid. Similarly, people become angry because they argue and people feel sad because they cry.

Most laymen would class this as nonsense, or begging the question 'Well, what makes you run, or argue, or cry?' But it went unchallenged for many years. Eventually the physiologist Walter Cannon attacked the argument by demonstrating that physiological changes were slower than had previously been believed. If the feeling of emotion *preceded* its physiological pattern, then the latter could not cause the former. And Cannon found no evidence that physiological activity differed from one emotional state to another. Finally, in a rather clever experiment, Cannon injected *adrenalin* into volunteers, but did not tell them what effect to expect. Volunteers failed to experience the increased arousal usually associated with a sudden rise in adrenalin.

Today, Cannon's theory, that emotions are not determined by physiological responses alone, is widely accepted and of course accords with common experience (not always a reliable guide).

We do not differentiate between emotional states solely on the basis of bodily changes. For example, the physiological upheavals which occur with fear (increased adrenalin, increased blood-sugar levels and respiration, blood-flow acceleration, stomach-wall and blood-vessel constriction, pupil-dilation) also attend anger and other forms of arousal. Physiological differences that do exist appear to be linked to the way what one might call 'undifferentiated' internal emotion is outwardly differentiated or *expressed*. When you express anger or hostility, the adrenals secrete a greater quantity of the hormone noradrenalin. When anger is inhibited and not expressed, the adrenals secrete increased amounts of adrenalin.

While bodily changes may determine the *intensity* of emotion, we use clues from our environment to identify its *quality*—that

*No difficulty guessing
what emotion
is being expressed here.*

is, which emotion it is. Assume for example that our emotional reactions were based solely on our physiological feedback such as increases in heart rate, dry mouth, high blood pressure, urinary frequency, nausea, vomiting, mild diarrhoea, sluggish light reflexes and so on. Most of us, without knowing the context in which this is all taking place (or the preceding circumstances) would probably explain this as the manifestation of some negative emotion. Actually, these are some of the more common physiological effects of marijuana smoking. Mental attitudes and social learning therefore have an important effect on our emotional state.

Mind over matter

Richard Lazarus recognised the importance of cognitive factors, and developed the 'way-we-see-things' standpoint into a 'cognitive-appraisal' theory of emotion. And Stanley Schachter and Jerome Singer conducted ingenious experiments to examine the idea that the way we regard an emotion-producing situation determines our emotional responses to it.[1]

Schachter and Singer made the rather vague concept of

'emotion' amenable to experimental investigation, pioneering the interaction or partial integration of elements from social psychology, cognitive processes and physiology in the process.

They found that by administering certain 'drugs', they could manipulate what people thought they were supposed to feel and therefore what they felt. Previous information about the effects of the 'drugs' appeared enough for volunteers actually to experience these effects, despite the fact that in some cases the 'drugs' were entirely inert substances. Although Schachter and Singer's study has yet to be successfully repeated (it has been criticised on methodological grounds), there is strong support for the theory that what you *believe* to be happening modifies organic and psychological functioning. Appraisal of both the meaning and seriousness of a situation is clearly important in determining the emotion felt.

'That's what eating ice cream does for you!' Now that you know the situation (see page 74), did you weigh it up correctly?

76

In our materialistic, rational societies many people dismiss the old ideas associated with 'mind over matter'. But much research suggests that attitudes and psychological make-up influence our physical well-being.

In Western society about half of all patients who consult physicians have symptoms originating largely in emotional disturbance. Emotional factors also impede recovery from physical illness. And organic illnesses such as tuberculosis, heart disease, diabetes and epilepsy may be intensified by emotional factors. This is why such efforts are made to help patients maintain a cheerful mood.

The emotional condition we call faith both kills and cures. Its curative powers have been proven, both historically and in contemporary medicine, by successful cases of faith-healing. The simple belief that pain will recede because of some real or imagined catalyst is often enough to do the trick. 'Placebo' pills, with no medicinal value, have cured people of incapacitating physical symptoms as well as mild ones. In one study by Beecher, more than 3,000 out of 4,500 adults were cured of severe headaches—thanks to placebos.[2] Beecher also reported that one in every three patients reported relief from ailments ranging from the common cold to multiple sclerosis. While injections of morphine relieved chronic pain in 65 per cent of cancer patients, placebo injections effectively helped 42 per cent—and placebos have no unwelcome side-effects.

Belief in authority and ability can even *reverse* pharmacological effects of drugs. A group of women were told that their medication would alleviate nausea during early pregnancy. Many women reported that 'morning sickness' had ceased. They had been given ipecacuanha, a drug which is normally used to induce vomiting.

Eastern religious disciplines have given us much insight into the techniques of 'mind over matter'.

The stiff upper lip, *sang froid* and all that

Quite apart from the 'mind over matter' aspect, our minds and our emotions are exceptionally powerful forces. Some features of emotional behaviour are positive, but others may interfere with adjustment and problem-solving or even incapacitate us. We have to find a means of tolerating emotional expression without suffering the damage caused by emotional excess.

This raises the question of emotional control, which remains a somewhat vexed question both in terms of practical and theoretical psychology. Western civilisation admires restraint. 'Don't lose your head', we say. But have we gone too far in seeking to suppress emotional expression? Emotional suppression is not always successful as, instead of being safely vented (as excess steam pressure is relieved by a boiler's safety valve) the emotion may express itself in distorted form or in illness (just as boilers may leak or even split).

The answer seems to lie in emotional control without emotional denial. When we experience our emotions without anxiety and guilt and accept them as natural, handling them in socially acceptable ways, then we are emotionally healthy.

Another scandalous police cover-up! Now that he is fully exposed, did you grasp what he was feeling? (see page 74)

Focus on aggression

As we have seen, emotions can activate, direct and accompany behaviour. They can also be goals in themselves—for example, sexual activity for the sake of pleasure. Aggression fits in with these concepts and it is reasonable to look upon it not only as behaviour, but as a powerful emotion. It underlines the link between feeling an emotion and expressing it as a behaviour.

Almost daily, news bulletins report murders, muggings and mass killings. What lies behind this aggressive behaviour? It is too simple just to put aggression down to single emotions such as anger and frustration.

What about personal responsibility, intent, the situation that causes it? Is it a matter of social labelling rather than behaviour in and of itself?

The core of an aggressive act is that it is an attempt to harm someone, either physically or verbally. Unpleasant emotions like pain, fear, anger and especially frustration often lead to aggressive feelings, but do not always instigate aggressive behaviour.

Can aggression be controlled? In search of the answer, psychologists have turned to the animal kingdom for some illumination. They have found, for example, that the more territory an animal commands, the less aggressive its behaviour is likely to be. Yet other studies show that animals are more aggressive when guarding their territory from within than when they are outside it. So psychologists looked more closely at the question of territory for further explanations.

Misinterpreted emotions: the man is joking, but the threat seems real enough to the dog.

Territorial ambitions

It is almost a 'human right' to defend ourselves against uninvited intrusion of our private world. Wars have resulted from hostile invasions of a country by foreigners. Street gangs guard their territory. We react with a certain amount of hostility to the stranger who moves 'uncomfortably' close on public transport, in shops—even in church. This is the basis of a popular theory on aggression supported by comparative psychologists and ethologists (who study animal behaviour in the wild for the lessons it has in human society).

Waterloo. The price of territorial ambition can be prohibitive.

Social learning and culture play an important part in how we define 'personal space'. When a North American talks to a stranger of the same sex, the distance between them is unlikely to be less than 20 inches. But Arab strangers of the same sex happily converse in closer proximity. For Americans, posture, eye-contact, touch, breath and sound level within the 20-inch limit is disconcerting—unless in intimate conversation with someone of the opposite sex.

While the parallels between human and animal 'sense of territory' are undeniably strong (see p. 7, Chapter 1), we humans are known to make certain allowances. For instance, more than four million foreigners are tolerated each year by the British during the summer. As tourists, rather than invaders, they are accepted—despite the fact that they have 'foreign ways', litter the streets and fill theatres and restaurants almost to the exclusion of their hosts.

'The territorial imperative', as it has been called, is an important factor in the roots of human aggression. But it does not account for it all.

Sigmund Freud was one of the first psychologists to develop the theory that humans are *instinctively* aggressive. When theorising about motivation and personality, he described two opposing basic human instincts. He called the instinct for growth and life by its Greek name *eros*, while *thanatos* was the death instinct. Since Freud assumed that *thanatos* required perpetual expression, he was pessimistic about removing aggression from human nature.

Freud saw the energy for the death instinct as being like water accumulating in a reservoir: the level would rise until it finally spilled over in some aggressive act. A 'safe' way in which aggression could be expressed was by means of *catharsis* (another Greek word, meaning purification or cleansing). In catharsis, the emotions are expressed in their full intensity through words, crying or other symbolic means.

Freud's theory, despite its poetic appeal, has gained little scientific support. In his later writings, Freud himself played down the importance of a death instinct. But 'innate aggression' is stressed in an ethological theory based on animal studies: Konrad Lorenz argued that aggression is a spontaneous, innate readiness to fight—a critical factor for survival. Yet animals rarely kill or injure others of the same species; only humans have lost the means of inhibiting aggression. We kill each other, and kill animals for pleasure. Alone in the animal world, human beings are threatened by their own aggression.

Eros, thanatos and catharsis? Freud would have been excited by this mixture of love, danger and symbolically expressed aggression.

Biological bases of aggression

The relationships between biochemistry and physiology and aggression are complex and unclear. The brain, hormonal factors and genetics have often emerged as contributory factors, and much research has been done on animals to shed light on physiologically-based aggression. In one notable experiment, the Spanish psychologist José Delgado stopped a charging bull in its tracks by radioing a message to electrodes implanted in its brain. More significantly, repeated experiences of this 'switching off' caused the animal to become permanently less aggressive.[3]

Likewise, certain drugs injected into a specific area of the brain in rats turned those which were aggressive into placid ones. A different drug injected into exactly the same brain site of normally placid rats induced them to turn on and kill mice. It is clear that to a great extent aggressive behaviour *is* linked to a specific function of the brain.

But there are different physiological patterns in different kinds of aggression. Researchers have found, for example, that particular aggressive behaviours in humans are often linked to brain disorders. Diseases of the limbic system and temporal lobe have been discovered in people with a history of senseless brutality and serious sexual assaults. It has also been conjectured that overly aggressive behaviour is caused by an extra 'y' chromosome in men, although as yet there is no firm evidence to support this idea. One thing is certain though: whether in animals or humans, males are characteristically more aggressive than females, which suggests some plausibility for the chromosome idea. Normal males have only one 'y'; and females have none. Hormonal differences might equally play a part however.

Maleness, territoriality, the authority of uniform all contribute to aggression between these two.

Learning to be aggressive

Another possible answer to the 'why' of aggression is that it is learned—the result of rewards, punishments, norms and models.

In an experiment carried out by Albert Bandura and colleagues,[4] groups of pre-school children were exposed to various aggressive models—an aggressive adult, a model of aggression on film, and cartoon aggressors. Other groups of children were shown non-aggressive models. The children were subsequently 'frustrated' by the experimenters and it was found that those who had observed aggressive models imitated many of the aggressive acts they had seen. The children who had not been exposed to aggressive models were less likely to be aggressive.

In later experiments, Bandura exposed pre-schoolers to models of aggressors being punished.[5] This resulted in the children who had seen the models punished displaying significantly less imitative aggression. He also showed that aggression was not simply a temporary performance. The children remembered specific patterns of aggression-provoking sequences used in previous testing. Aggression once learnt is not easily unlearnt.

Bandura presented his work as a *social learning* theory which states that aggression may be caused by either aversive experiences or the promise of rewards. While most psychoanalysts regard frustration as the only kind of aversive experience strong enough to provoke aggression, behaviourists like Bandura believe that we learn to react aggressively to all kinds of anxiety-provoking situations. We can also learn to use aggression for our own ends. The child who lashes out in order to procure a toy is an obvious example.

Social learning theory rejects the idea of our having aggressive *drives* or *instincts*; and *catharsis* is also dismissed.

Expressing aggression: good or bad?

Bandura's ideas are well supported experimentally. Studies show that giving either adults or children the opportunity to aggress *encourages* more aggression. In one study, children were allowed to aggress against one of their number who had frustrated them. Their aggressive feelings remained unchanged afterwards. The catharsis theory would predict that their feelings of aggression would be reduced. It appears to make sense. We 'let off steam' or 'let ourselves go' by crying, laughing, shouting—and we feel better. Yet research shows that this process does not apply to aggressive *behaviour*.

On the other hand, Bandura's social learning theory does not cover all possibilities. The theory begins to strain at the seams when we ask why people from similar environments, with similar life experience, can vary so greatly in their expression of aggression. In short, the theory fits experimental findings rather well, but much more work is needed to match it up to the complexities of actual behaviour in our city streets.

The mass media and violence

Learning to live with the instruments of violence (above); and (below) learning how to stay alive at the receiving end.

For much longer than the term 'mass media' has been in use, there has been a commonly-held opinion that what is sold to us as entertainment can give rise to anti-social behaviour. Horror comics, films, radio, pop music, early 'penny dreadfuls' and chap-books, bearpits, even the minstrels and troubadours, have all been blamed for social evils. In this century, the prime target for criticism is television.

No one can deny that television is a violent medium. Factual programmes such as newscasts and documentaries highlight death and violence. Entertainment programmes are laden with killings and fist fights. Growing opinion suggests that apparently increasing rates of violence, particularly amongst young people, are related to this bloody medium.

The facts are clear enough. American children spend more time watching television than they spend in school. In each hour of viewing they will witness somewhere between one and eight killings, not to mention numerous fights and examples of cruelty or torture. Research evidence, although not yet conclusive, suggests that this level of exposure affects young people.

In the early 1970s, special studies were conducted at the instigation of the Surgeon General of America. The final (five-volume) report argued that a 'preliminary and tentative' link between television-watching and violent behaviour had been revealed. Most social scientists involved in these studies are convinced that the governments of Western nations should take action to reduce the amount of televised aggression.

But the more intensively these questions are studied, the more confusing are the answers. Experimental studies show that televised violence can produce aggression *in the laboratory*. But this is a demonstration of a process, not proof that the process is operating in our cities. And although survey research repeatedly shows that aggressive children (particularly boys) tend to seek out and enjoy violent television, correlations do not necessarily equate with causality. It is possible that some other factor causes these boys to be aggressive *and* to seek out violent television programmes.

So strong is the lure of television that we have to take it with us: do we swallow its values, hook, line and sinker, as well?

The evidence for what television does to children's behaviour is conflicting—but something that plays so large a part in our lives cannot be without effect on them.

The problem is that while surveys tell us about life as it is, they cannot provide evidence of causality; and while laboratory experiments tell us about causality, they cannot be generalised to life as it is. A small number of 'field experiments' have been conducted that combine the strengths of both approaches. Such studies are extremely costly and difficult to mount. And the results have only added to the confusion.

One study, by the American psychologists Feshbach and Singer, supports the catharsis hypothesis—watching televised violence has no effect or *reduces actual aggression*. Another, by Milgram, indicates that adults imitate anti-social acts seen on television. And yet another study, involving kindergarten children, suggests that watching televised violence not only increases aggression among some children but also increases *pro-social* play among others.

Most British psychologists who have studied mass media argue that the results of all studies, taken together, are equivocal. And, they point out, the question, 'Does television cause violence?' is naïve. In order to understand the roots of violence and aggression, we must understand society and the place of violence within it. To emphasise the role of one facet of society—television—is to risk missing some other more important factors.

Can violence in society be prevented?

In order to prevent violence, it would be necessary to change our societies almost beyond recognition. Violence is a cultural form, acceptable in some situations, prohibited in others. Fight in the boxing ring and you may be honoured by society, fight in the street outside and you may be arrested. Many of our leading statesmen were trained killers during their younger days. A man will be given national honours for killing several hundred adults and children on a bombing raid, but be imprisoned for attacking his wife or child.

Clearly there are no simple solutions to the problems raised by our violent and aggressive natures. But we do know that some solutions work for some kinds of violence. Improving social conditions reduces violence within the family. Among the near-starving working classes of Victorian Britain, wife-beating was commonplace. It is also clear that violent crime statistics vary from city to city according to the density and quality of housing.

But what of the quiet, spacious suburbs where the murder of a spouse is not unknown? And why is there so much vandalism in new, carefully planned towns? Since the Thirties, some psychologists have argued that violence is a natural consequence of frustration. Others accept the social learning theory of aggression, while yet others point to the possibility of an aggressive instinct and the importance of catharsis.

Frustration? Urban squalor? Social learning? Innate aggressiveness? No single answer suffices in Northern Ireland.

No single explanation can yet be applied to all aspects of felt aggression or aggressive behaviour. Perhaps what we see as one kind of behavioural manifestation actually masks several different human characteristics. If this is the case—and it now seems rather likely—then all the theories are probably right some of the time. Unfortunately, this also means that they are all wrong some of the time. Only time and diligent scientific research will clarify these critically important questions. And in a nuclear age some people argue that time is running out.

7   'I am that I am'

Personality is certainly a common enough word. We speak of nice or strong 'personalities' when describing people, either as a simple synonym or, more often, reserving it for those with 'star appeal'—celebrities from stage and screen, popular politicians, bright and cheeky school fellows. 'Personality plus' is something we'd all like to have. But none of these everyday uses of the word captures the psychological concept of personality.

To the psychologist, 'personality' is the sum total of ways in which a person reacts to, and interacts with, other people and the environment. Personality in this sense is the integration of attitudes, values, habits, physical characteristics, interests, abilities and so on. Clearly, the psychologist cannot say, 'John has a lot of personality, Lisa has no personality'. The scientific study of personality is the study of the whole person, and we are all that.

Personality needs people

The word itself derives from the Greek *persona*—a mask. A mask is not the true self but a representation (true or false) *displayed for the sake of others.* Although psychologists today do not regard personality as a mask to hide the true self, all agree that other people contribute to the development of the individual personality and even to its transient manifestations (as in 'He is a different person when he is with her ...'). Without other people to react to, and to react to us, we would have no meaningful identity, and without identity personality becomes a meaningless concept.

We each have a unique personality, and psychologists agree that three factors contribute to its formation—heredity, culture, and individual experience. Each of these three factors is played up or played down by one theory or another. Some argue that heredity—our biological, genetically-fixed characteristics—accounts for the greater part of personality. Others admit that, although our physical appearance is largely shaped by heredity and this probably influences personality, the social environment and culture in which we live makes the greatest contribution. A third group allows for the other two sources of influence, but believes that our unique experience, and how we interpret and use it, shapes personality growth.

These theories are not easy to put to the test since we are

The clown may be a 'personality' without revealing the real personality behind the persona or mask of his make-up.

dealing with real people who live just as long as the scientists studying them. Psychologists cannot, for example, practise selective breeding in order to study the contribution of heredity. And clearcut answers are sometimes difficult to attain because they carry political overtones that excite public concern.

Take the question of intelligence and race. Few dispute that American blacks used to score lower on Intelligence Quotient tests than American whites. But why was this so? Some argue that there is a genetic predisposition. Others point out that the intelligence tests are biased towards the white culture (and design black intelligence tests which neatly reverse the black/white difference!). A third group points to the cultural deprivation of blacks in America as compared to whites. A scientific question has thus become a political one, generating 'great heat but little light'.

The nature–nurture debate

In terms of our development, how much 'personality' is attributable to what *nature* provides and how much to the kind of *nurture* we receive?

Badges of security or the trappings of insecurity?

Two 17th-century British philosophers are often credited with planting the seeds not only of the nature/nurture debate, but also of contemporary psychology as well. Thomas Hobbes argued that humans are guided by their inherited instincts from the moment they come into the world. There can be little individual control over their destiny. On the other hand John Locke fathered the *tabula rasa* theory which holds that the mind of a newborn baby is a blank slate on which any impression can be imprinted. By finding the right method of instruction we will be shaped this or that way.

Nature *vs* nurture or environment *vs* heredity has in past years often been presented as an either/or position although these days it is rarely so stated. Rather, psychologists are keen on the *relative* importance of heredity and environment in the shaping of our behaviour. Environmentalists agitate for the scientific study of the environment, simply because the environment can be manipulated, thereby affecting behavioural outcome. Predeterminists, in support of the heredity viewpoint, argue that changes in the environment are unimportant because individuals with different genetic inheritances will respond to environmental manipulations in different ways. The scientific evidence adduced in the nature/nurture debate is in any case open to a number of different interpretations.

In one study, developmental psychologists tracked more than a hundred infants from birth to adolescence.[1] They concluded that basic temperamental characteristics evident soon after birth had dominated their development throughout the years. These characteristics included general mood, adaptability to the environment, quietness, fretfulness, persistence, activity, acceptance of new objects and people. As the children approached adolescence, the psychologists were able to predict, to a significant degree, the personality 'make-up' of those subjects. This was presented as evidence that the biological processes dominated personality growth.

Not twins, but unmistakably from the same genetic stock.

Environmentalists disagreed. They reasoned that the parents of these babies would have reinforced recognisable characteristics, which in their developed form would, therefore, be due not to heredity but to learning.

Walter Mischel, of Stanford University, firmly opposed the notion that personality is based on heredity and the result of innate traits. He has championed the idea that our behaviour in any situation may change dramatically because of previous experiences and that a change in the situation (or environment) would produce dramatic changes in 'personality'. Even the way we conduct ourselves can change under specific circumstances.

In arguments about the primacy of heredity or environment (or the chicken and the egg), people tend to be shackled to prejudices.

Over 50 years ago, a classic experiment by Hartshorne and May[2] foreshadowed the kind of observation that was to lead Mischel to this view. The *honesty* of schoolchildren was recorded in an attempt to find out how many of them would cheat given the chance. The results showed that there were no clearly definable cheaters and non-cheaters. Children varied in their honesty from test to test. It all depended on elements of risk involved, the effort required and what their friends were seen to be doing.

Although 'honesty' in childhood is malleable, ethical behaviour becomes more firmly established as we grow older. Environmentalists point to the power of society and its sub-cultures as a major factor in this long-term hardening process. Values, ethics and attendant attitudes are all influenced by those around us. We are *socialised*, say these environmentalists, into particular cultures and sub-cultures and there is no way of diverting this powerful shaping process. Others—and in particular the Swiss psychologist Jean Piaget—have detected a relationship between cognitive development and the understanding of moral issues which they say satisfactorily explains this process.

Unique experiences are occasionally potent enough to alter personality growth. Major behavioural change has been brought about by events such as religious conversion, illness, death of a close one or financial turmoil.

Their fluid childhood values and attitudes are 'set' into adult patterns by the particular sub-culture in which they grow up.

Perhaps the most relevant and practical debate on heredity *vs* environment has focussed in recent years on the issue of intelligence. Here the evidence is particularly hard to interpret—which has not prevented people taking firm stands on one side or the other.

Intelligence and personality

It is easy enough for a layman to say in broad terms what 'intelligence' is, and even to distinguish between this apparently desirable quality and mere 'cleverness' on the one hand and 'wisdom' on the other. But after a century of investigation and argument, it would be difficult to find a majority of psychologists anywhere who would agree on a definition of the term. In spite of this the business of intelligence and aptitude testing has become the main area of contact between the psychology profession and the public. The interpretation of test results has in turn become a topic of major controversy, with important implications for social and educational policies and, ultimately, for the way our societies are governed.

Intelligence testing began in France in the early years of this century. The Paris education authority, strongly imbued with the 'success/failure' ethic that still characterises most Western-style education and with the compulsion to categorise which marks all developed bureaucracies, wanted a means of identifying children likely to do badly in their schools. The man they consulted, Alfred Binet, devised a tool brilliantly suited to the task. Binet's tests, consisting of a series of questions of increasing difficulty, were designed to uncover ability in various mental processes. It must be emphasised that they were not intended to give an absolute measurement of 'intelligence' (as length, say, is absolutely measured by a calibrated tape) but to provide a comparative and discriminatory indication of divergence from a social norm.

What happens, even in modern developments of the test like the so-called *Stanford–Binet*, is that the performance in these tests of a large sample of the population is called 'standard' and individual performances are compared with it. The resulting figure, called the *Intelligence Quotient* (IQ), is written in percentage terms—an IQ of 125 means a performance 25 per cent better than the average in that test (as much care as possible is taken to compare like with like). Given uniform test conditions and, more important, uniform social and cultural backgrounds among those tested, the IQ does give a good general indication of how children will perform in school. But a disturbed night, or being a non-native speaker of the language of the test, or low expectations or poor encouragement to achievement by parents, can lead to an entirely mistaken view of a child's potential.

This might not matter so much were it not that IQ has come to have a powerfully concrete meaning for teachers, parents, employers and so on. Their expectations, based on this misinterpretation, can be shown to exert a decisive influence on the subsequent performance of children labelled with these particular magic figures. This is something in the nature of a self-fulfilling prophecy: a low scorer will be expected to perform badly (and

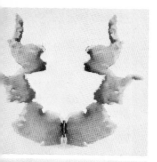

may find good performance going unrecognised because of this) and will eventually expect himself to perform badly.

In an ideal world everybody would agree that the only quality measured by intelligence tests is the ability to do intelligence tests. Perhaps then, the damaging categorisation of people into ups and downs, ins and outs, goods and bads, might be abandoned. But the world is not ideal, and people like to know where they stand in relation to other people. Most societies will in any case insist that reasons of state or social policy necessitate the comparative assessment of 'human resources'. Bureaucrats will always wish to discriminate between, say, the potentially useful and not so useful, between the innovative and the conservative, disruptive and docile, or any other pair of distinguishing characteristics.

Personality tests

In these circumstances much more comprehensively informative testing is required, and *personality tests* are now generally in use which seek to identify all sorts of qualities other than 'intelligence'. Some of these tests are of the question-and-answer or choice type, like the *Minnesota Multiphasic Personality Inventory* (MMPI), in which a large number of subjective statements ('I never worry about my looks', 'I often feel things are not real') require 'true', 'false' or 'can't say' responses. Trained testers can derive a general impression of personality from these, with indications of the kind and severity of disturbances and distortions.

Other tests are *projective*—the subject imposes his own ideas on to a given verbal outline or picture which is, designedly, ambiguous or neutral in itself. The *Rorschach* uses ink-blots, the *Thematic Apperception Test* (TAT) pictures of single or paired people. The themes developed by the subject in talking about these can be analysed and used to provide a guide to his or her conformity to or divergence from a 'normal' personality profile.

How normal is 'normal'?

Rorschach test cards (above): see what ideas come into your head while you look at them—and then think about the ideas!

All theories of personality depend on defining 'normality'. This is not possible in social terms except as a function of a particular time and place—'this is what people ordinarily do in this country in 1979' is not the same as 'what people ordinarily did in Siam in 1239'. Psychologists are able to use a more consistent definition even if it is a negative one: someone so mentally impaired that he cannot function in his society is *abnormal*. Even then there can be no clear dividing line between normal and abnormal, only an attempt to place somebody somewhere on a scale whose extremes are normal and abnormal.

'Normal' covers a broad range, even in terms of the functioning of our bodies. In his work on individual biochemical differences, R. J. Williams[3] was able to demonstrate great variations in the size, location and operation of internal organs and neural structures. According to Williams, 'normal' healthy young adults may have heart-beat rates ranging from 50 to 105 beats per minute, 'normal' heart-pumping capacities ranging from 3.15 to 11.9 quarts per minute.

If a thyroid gland is overactive, a person may well become irritable, nervous and insomniac. If, for any reason, the gland becomes underactive, the same person becomes lethargic and unemotional. When the proven range of biochemical differences are combined with the enormous range of unique personal experiences, it is virtually impossible to find 'normal' baselines for human behaviour. Add to this cultural and sub-cultural influences and we can see how complex definitions of normality are. For example, what would be outrageously 'abnormal' behaviour in our culture—public masturbation—is acceptable among the Ashanti of West Africa.

Not outside the bounds of 'normality' in this context; but a few miles away in another suburb of the same city she would be thought outrageously abnormal.

Consistency

The fact that we are inconsistent in our behaviour is consistent in itself. Most people can be both generous *and* mean, sociable *and* shy, friendly *and* hostile. We know this about ourselves and yet most of us quite happily label people on the basis of some obvious characteristic that we think predominates. Somebody we know is 'always' happy, sad, cheerful, witty or whatever. What we mean is that she is consistent in her behaviour towards us (and if she isn't we say she seemed 'off form' today or 'not quite herself').

But we don't know how she behaves towards others. The miserable cop on traffic duty—the one who never has a good word for anybody—might well be a comedian in the bar-room, a samaritan at the local youth club and an intellectual amongst the members of his chess club. There is also very little consistency from one situation to another. Under different conditions we behave as if we were different people.

Typecasting people

In the remainder of this chapter, we will consider four dominant personality theories: types and traits; humanistic; psycho-analytic; and behaviourist.

When a scientist scrutinises an object under a microscope, his or her first move is usually to classify it as of a certain *type*. This laboratory approach was applied to the study of personality. Known as the 'trait approach', it was based on the idea that we have stable characteristics in our make-up. Kretschmer and Sheldon would certainly have classified someone short and plump as an *endomorph*—and therefore likely to be sociable, relaxed and placid. A tall, thin friend, on the other hand, would be restrained, quiet and self-conscious in company with fellow *ectomorphs*. Most people may be said to be a mixture of these two types. But although physique probably does have a certain influence on personality, the relationship is less direct than this theory implies. Many other factors must be taken into account.

In the 1930s, Gordon Allport argued that in order to understand the mosaic of personality, it is necessary to break it down into its component parts. He and his colleagues listed almost 18,000 expressions for human characteristics or traits. Over the years they reduced the list to an assortment of relatively stable traits such as kindness, meanness, spitefulness, consider-ateness, gentleness, loudness and so on. They then constructed special tests to measure these traits, and by administering them to large numbers of people, it became possible to build 'personality norms'.

It was Carl Jung who really pioneered the classification of people into 'psychological types.' He suggested two major classifications: *extroverts* and *introverts*.[4] Introverts are with-

Extrovert or introvert? The clues are decisive.

drawn, cautious and non-sociable, and these tendencies are significantly increased during stressful encounters. Extroverts are the opposite—outgoing, impulsive, warm people who actively seek the company of others—especially in times of stress.

Jung's approach was later extensively researched and developed by the two eminent psychologists Cattell and Eysenck, both of whom developed scales to measure the dimension of introversion-extroversion. Eysenck's measures, for example, uncover individual differences in terms of how much we need others as a source of reward or even to shape our behaviour.

The internal-external personality metaphor has been the focus of a good deal of serious attention in recent years, and the evidence of research suggests that there are, indeed, as the saying has it, 'two kinds of people in the world'. 'Internal' people feel that rewards for their actions depend solely on their own behaviour. 'Externals' see rewards occurring as independently of their actions—and as being due rather to environmental factors. Internals tend to avoid situations where they may lose control of how they are rewarded. They resist social pressures more, are less conformist and more independent than externals. They take their decisions more seriously and tend to concentrate more on skills, rather than on chance, to influence outcomes.

Round pegs in round holes?

A useful application of the 'personality type' approach is found in personnel selection and vocation guidance. 'Norms' for particular types of work have been produced, and they go far beyond such obvious views as that intelligence and extroversion are essential ingredients for good salesmanship. The main utility of the trait approach has been its success as an applied science in selection and classification. As a theory it is an improvement on the commonsense use of 'global' personality stereotypes. But it is largely a pragmatic approach with little explanatory power. Personality is enigmatic and complex, and we are almost all 'extro-intro' 'internal-external' mixtures, depending upon how we feel, whom we are with and where we are.

Being your own thing

Not what is meant by 'the actualisation of self'—but doing his own thing all the same.

An entirely different orientation to personality is maintained by 'organismic-field' theorists, such as Goldstein, Maslow, Rogers, Jourard and Berne. They emphasise our potential for self-destruction, self-development, freedom of choice and capacity for change. The implicit message is that there are values in living that we know from our own experiences and observations are precious and enhancing: expressiveness, enjoyment, emotional responsiveness, sensory awareness, spontaneity, self-support, compassion, creativity and so on.

To these *humanists*, or *existentialists* as they are often called, the basis of individual consistency is the 'actualisation of self'—the process of striving to find and realise one's own potential. This is often achieved by exploring, then experiencing, those factors which stop, block or frustrate our personality growth.

Abraham Maslow, a major figure in the field, looked on the unconscious as the seat of the greatest happiness, creativity and good. Unconscious drives propel us in our quest for wholeness and truth; we have an 'active will towards health, an impulse towards growth, or towards the actualisation of human potentialities'. 'Peak experiences' such as sex, religion and certain types of music can bring out an awareness of one's 'self', one's 'body' and one's 'being'. According to Maslow, personality should be judged solely within this very positive frame of reference.

The ideal self

Carl Rogers, another pioneer in this theory, argued that we are all capable of moulding our own personalities.[5] He has also emphasised the importance of inner experiences. To Rogers, *how* we see, feel and interpret events is the key to understanding the development of personality and behaviour. Each of us needs to appraise our own personalities, without denying our faults or weaknesses, strengths or capacities. We should set up an 'ideal self', making a conscious effort to be the person we would really like to be. Self-acceptance is the first step in a change towards the better, and then we must be able to express our feelings more directly to others.

Unfortunately, most of us have a tendency to see ourselves in terms of other people's values rather than those of our own. This 'social self' is often at odds with our 'ideal self'. To Rogers, the wider the discrepancy, the greater the likelihood of being psychologically disturbed. Like Maslow, Rogers has elaborated a theory which underlines personal action and growth.

Personal responsibility and growth are key conceptions in humanistic psychology, which has become a most prominent theoretical trend in recent years. Perhaps this is due to the growing interest in the self—especially among young people. With its possibilities for 'self-awareness', love, creativity, and caring (dominant themes in religious practices and mysticism), it reinforces the notion of individual experience, as opposed to physical events, as the basis of reality.

The analyst's way

Sigmund Freud—whose name is, to most laymen, almost synonymous with investigation of the mind—is still regarded as having made a unique contribution to psychology. He did not regard himself solely as a clinician but also as a social thinker. Today, although his dominance has long since been reduced, his theories continue to have an enormous influence on current psychology and particularly on *psychoanalysis* as a treatment of psychological problems.

Freud's critics are quick to point out that many of his original thoughts were based on his observations of a smallish band of middle-class Viennese patients—living of course in the late 19th century. Therefore his sweeping generalisations about human behaviour should not be taken too seriously. Indeed, there remains very little evidence that Freud was anywhere near correct in his theories.

Having said that, our comprehension of the way we are and behave as humans probably owes more to Sigmund Freud than to any of his fellow investigators into mental health. He made a very big something out of almost nothing—the small change of psychological observation that others had handled before him but not bothered to count, like slips of the tongue and hysterical paralysis. His special genius was to fit such occurrences into a psychological framework that made logical sense. It spurred him into defining the unconscious and what was for him the powerhouse of personality—irrational motivation. Freud's perspectives were profound. They changed the way in which societies at large look at and deal with child-rearing, formal education, sex, mental illness and crime.

Sigmund Freud and his followers developed a theory which emphasised sex and conflict as basic forces motivating behaviour. The roots of adult personality are to be found in early childhood experience; and the origins of our fears, anxieties and psychopathologies should be traced back to early-life traumas.

This is Freud's theory of *psychosexual stages of development*.[6] He divided growth into five major stages of personality development, each dominated by sexual urges. These sexual forces, known as *libido*, comprise most of the ways in which we satisfy ourselves through bodily stimulation. If libidinal drives are frustrated, or over-indulged at any stage, normal progression to the next stage is hindered and conflict results. Freud called this *fixation* at a particular stage.

The first psychosexual stage noted by Freud was *oral*; it is the period when the mouth is our primary source of stimulation. During the oral stage, infants and children derive great pleasure

*'But Florence is
a girl's name.'*

from thumb-sucking which fulfils no basic organic need. An oral fixation is held by Freudians to lead to later drug abuse, overeating or lesser evils such as 'verbal diarrhoea' and sarcasm.

Next is the *anal* stage. This centres around the elimination of faeces and pleasures associated with the retention of them. Since social norms regulate the elimination of excrement, many of the child's natural urges have to be suppressed. In societies which insist on harsh and early toilet-training, *anal fixation* is likely to occur frequently.

In the *phallic* stage, children explore and stimulate their own bodies, especially the genitalia.

During the *latency* stage the child's sexual interests (until now related largely to parents and family) 'go underground'. They re-emerge in the *genital* stage with the development of 'normal' sexuality, directed towards people outside the family.

Freud maintained that human personalities have unique qualities thanks to the *id*, the *ego* and the *superego*. These entirely theoretical constructions are thought to handle fundamental drives (like *eros* and *thanatos*) in various ways. Freud envisaged a continuous battle between the warring *id* and *superego*, with the *ego* acting like a modern-day 'shuttle diplomat' and moderating the outcome. The *id* is the natural habitat for sex, aggression and other hedonistic or animal-like drives (the *libido*). The *superego* is the repository of the conscience and good, quelling socially unacceptable drives.

Lifelong growth

Most neo-Freudians agree that personality is more or less fixed early on in life. Nevertheless, divergent views emerged under the analytic umbrella and had a marked impact on latter-day psychoanalytic thought. Carl Jung and Erik Erikson have both been instrumental in this regard.

Jung disagreed with Freud's sexual theories. He believed in lifelong personality growth rather than one centred on early childhood. Jung was fascinated by the influence on the individual of the *collective unconscious*: he assumed that each person inherits the unconscious material from previous generations. He therefore encouraged the exploration of the effects of parapsychological phenomena on personality growth. To this end, he undertook extensive studies of the occult, ritual, religion, magic and mythology. Interestingly enough, Jung's influence today is far greater in the creative arts than in professional psychology.

Erikson, on the other hand, developed the idea of critical stages in his approach to personality growth.[7] He formulated eight such stages, ranging from infancy to old age. According to Erikson, we all face specific crises, which, if resolved easily, make for wholesome personality development. Perhaps the most popular of his 'crisis' notions is that of *identity* in adolescence. Emerging into adulthood can be a terrifying and disorienting experience for the average adolescent. Successful resolution of identity problems ensures smooth and continuous personality growth.

The search for identity in adolescence can lead you up some bizarre side-tracks.

The behavioural approach

Behaviourists, social-learning theorists and *environmentalists* ascribe personality to the interplay of environmental, interpersonal and personal factors. Personality differences are generally regarded by them as the result of personal experience and changes in the conditions of learning. They believe that personality is malleable.

Henry Murray, schooled originally in the psychoanalytic mould, came to feel that Freud's biological instincts were too narrow in scope. Humans have differing needs which shape personality development. Prominent among these needs are: the domination of others and/or deference to authority and control; the achievement of excellence; friendship or need for affection; autonomy; play; and understanding. Unlike Freud, Murray emphasised the importance of the *environment* as a determinant of personality. A web of social factors influences the personality in particular ways (new friends, for example, are said to push or 'press' us towards satisfying our need for affection).

Rewarding relationships

To Harry Sullivan, the effects of human relations are paramount in the shaping of personality. His *interpersonal* theory is built on the impact on a growing human being of direct, remembered or even imagined relationships. Sullivan sees rewarding relationships as essential for favourable personality development.

Behaviourists look upon personality growth as a result of the interaction between *behaviour* in the physical world and whatever inner controlling conditions exist. The general heading 'behaviourist' covers several quite disparate approaches, however. Skinner, for example, would argue for almost total control of the personality by the environment. Such a position leaves little scope for free will or the interior dynamics assumed by Jung or Freud (one of the reasons why his book *Walden Two* has—to Skinner's apparent surprise—generated so much hostility: it describes a society in which everybody is conditioned into harmony with others and the society itself). Yet, in common with the other major personality theories encompassed in psychology, the behaviourist approach, whether total or modified, has contributed far more towards an understanding of the whole person than the 'commonsense' but superficial stereotypes often proposed as a more 'natural' approach to problems of personality.

Why theorise?

Indeed, you might well wonder what use personality theories could be in an area with so much conflicting evidence. The theories have in fact several practical implications and uses: they can tell us about likely behaviour in specified situations; they can tell us about different general types of people and what factors go into the constitution of these types; and most importantly, personality theory can help provide personal guidelines for living and improving the quality of one's own life. In practical terms from the professional point of view, personality theory is also essential to the methodology of psychological testing—one of the most successful applications of psychology to date. It has proved its value in increasing not only the efficiency of selection for tasks (its best-known application) but also the ease and comfort with which individuals can adapt to and fulfil themselves in an environment that seems at best neutral and at times actually hostile to the development of 'personality' at all. When there is a gross mismatch between personality and psychological environment, the expression of the conflict in the individual's behaviour can take alarming or tragic forms. The so-called 'nervous breakdown', which may be incapacitating or even responsible indirectly for the death of someone suffering from it, can often be traced to such conflict. 'Shell-shock', alcoholism, 'tics' and so on may also be expressions of a square peg personality finding itself in an intractably round psychological hole. Chapter 8 will discuss some of these deviant conditions more fully.

8   Going off the rails

When we have a sore throat, headache, running nose or muscular pains, we know that our doctor will probably diagnose 'a touch of flu'. Even if a malignant tumour is detected, the prognosis may not be good, but it is nevertheless identifiable.

But what of psychological pathology? How is it identified, what constitutes it, and how is it treated?

Dogmatic attitudes and cynical beliefs do much to sustain a fear of mental illness and behavioural disturbance, but the innate mysteriousness of the conditions and their causes is also, for people with a strong sense of 'normality', very worrying. Mental hospitals and institutions are thought of as 'loony-bins', 'nut-houses' or 'funny-farms', their inmates laughed at, scorned, rejected or isolated, the families and friends of patients made to feel disgraced or ashamed because we are afraid of 'madness'.

'You're driving me crazy . . .'

Most of us have seen someone whose public behaviour is grossly abnormal and eye-catching. And behaviour that is obviously odd presents us with the only observable evidence of abnormality or pathology. Yet it is often difficult to decide for sure when someone's behaviour is bizarre: not all aberrations from 'normal' fall into the description 'mad'. For instance, you may have a usually warm and outgoing friend who is becoming progressively withdrawn and suspicious. You may know somebody who has had a major setback at work and does not appear to be capable of readjusting. Perhaps you feel that they both need help, even though you would not dream of labelling them 'insane' or even—popular but too-often misapplied word—'neurotic'.

Is abnormality then just a matter of degree? Is it in the eye of the beholder? Who decides formally that someone is mad, or abnormal, or in need of psychological help? How does the diagnostic process work except as a matter of opinion? It will help if we consider two methods of looking at abnormality, and how psychologists derive their diagnostic criteria from them.

Bad for mankind

There is a so-called *evolutionary* definition of abnormal behaviour which describes it as 'maladaptive for the individual and ultimately for mankind as a species'. This definition can be

*Is this 'abnormality'—
or just a sensible
adaptation to a messy
set of conditions?*

*The once universal
'medical model' of
mental illness
dictated a typically
'hospital' approach
to its treatment.*

extended by the argument that behaviour is abnormal if it interferes with a person's—or a society's—chances of complete well-being, and leans heavily on 'health' as defined by the World Health Organisation in 1960: 'a state of complete physical, mental and social well-being and not merely the absence of disease and infirmity'.

According to the evolutionary definition, things like petty crime, cheating and cruelty are *abnormal* since they lessen people's chances of health. The fact that they are very common is not considered relevant in arriving at this conclusion.

Uncommon is abnormal

The *statistical* definition of abnormality classifies pathological behaviour by setting the standards of the particular society we live in against the way we as individuals act. According to this definition, very uncommon behaviour is abnormal; 'normality' and conformity to 'just the way things are' are equated. Even so, it is a flexible standard: a genius may be regarded as so 'different' as to be 'mad'—but a soldier who conforms to a common standard of killing everybody not dressed in the same clothes as he is wearing is accepted as perfectly normal. In some 'primitive' cultures it is common and acceptable for people to go into the trance-like emotional state that Western psychiatrists associate with catatonic schizophrenia.[1] Who is right?

Many psychologists and psychiatrists adopt a strictly pragmatic approach: if anyone comes to them seeking help, that is enough to be regarded as a candidate for therapy. Labels such as 'abnormal' may then be seen as unnecessary: the goal of therapy is not simply to get rid of odd behaviour, but to foster the fullest development and most wholesome awareness possible for each human being.

Such an approach does not help to diagnose actual mental illness, which is not necessarily the same as abnormality. Somebody has actually to *decide* whether the subject is mentally ill or not.

For many years this decision conformed to the 'medical model' built into psychiatry. Mental disturbances, in this model, are thought of as primarily caused by genetic or organic malfunction; abnormal behaviour is therefore a symptom of underlying disease; diseases are treated in hospitals by doctors. So for a long time such matters were left strictly in the hands of the psychiatric profession (that is, to those with traditional medical qualifications).

This approach to mental illness has come in for severe criticism from radical psychiatrists like R. D. Laing[2] and Thomas Szasz.[3] Laing has attacked and criticised the traditional concept of mental illness, psychiatric wards and mental hospitals, electro-convulsive shock therapy, the use of drugs in psychiatry, and the authoritarianism of traditional psychotherapy. Instead of seeing abnormal behaviour as the result of a person's past history or disease, Laing regards it as being caused by the current breakdown of his or her ability to interact and adjust. Szasz believes that the relationship between a hospital pyschiatrist and a patient is like that of master and slave rather than physician and adult patient.

It could well be, this 'radical' school argues, that so-called 'mental illness' is simply a healthy response to a sick society. Instead of treating the 'mentally ill' as passive patients, they feel that patients should themselves assume some active degree of responsibility for the management of their behaviour. Some psychiatrists see 'mental illness' simply as deviant behaviour. Sometimes 'mental illness' may not be even deviant behaviour but only a functional category invented or maintained by the expectations of society and mental health practitioners.

'If I say you're insane, you're insane!'
In a notable challenge to the conventional diagnosis and treatment of mental illness in 1973, David Rosenhan and 12 of his associates used false identities and had themselves 'committed' to various mental hospitals in America.[4] They falsified certain information about their supposed complaints ('I hear voices, unclean voices...'), but everything else about their past histories and current circumstances was truthfully reported.

What used to happen to the mentally ill in former times: restraints in Bedlam (Bethlem Royal Hospital)

At 11 out of 12 hospitals, the would-be patients were diagnosed as 'schizophrenic' and committed to psychiatric wards on the strength of their simulated 'abnormalities'. Once inside, however, Rosenhan and his colleagues stopped simulating psychiatric symptoms—each behaved as normally as possible in every way. Yet despite their public 'show' of sanity, the pseudo-patients remained undetected. Each was eventually discharged with a diagnosis of 'schizophrenia in remission' after having been hospitalised for an average of 19 days. At no time did any hospital staff member realise that an admissions error had been made or that a perfectly normal person was being kept in an asylum for the insane. It was left to husbands, wives and colleagues to secure their release.

The staff of one American hospital which heard about Rosenhan's study staunchly professed that such errors of judgment could not have happened at their establishment. Rosenhan put their claims to the test by stating that one or more 'impostors' would apply for admission to their hospital during the following three months. Each of the 193 patients admitted during this period was systematically rated by the staff, and 19 were classified by both a psychiatrist and a staff member as fakes.

A total of 41 patients were judged to be 'pseudo' by at least one staff member. The number of actual pseudo-patients sent to the hospital by Rosenhan was . . . nil.

This is undoubtedly (unless you are cynical enough to think Rosenhan's group was, indeed, mad) a most shocking indictment of certain 'medical model' techniques of hospital admission and diagnosis—and hardly likely to allay common fears and apprehensions about the possibility of being wrongly sent to a mental institution. But, reassuringly, there has been a major change of ideas within psychology and psychiatry about concepts such as 'normality' and 'insanity' even in the past few years. Contemporary mental health specialists are working on fresh and effective approaches toward diagnosis and treatment.

Take it away with a pill

Psychological discomfort can arise in many ways—guilt over keeping a mistress, tension in times of crisis, hopelessness in times of loss, anxiety over non-promotion. One way of getting rid of it may be simply to give up what causes guilt or anxiety;

The kind of conditions to which tranquillisers have come to be the too-popular answer

another to accept the comforts of religion in loss and crisis. But nobody *wants* to give up mistress or job, and religion is not these days the powerful solace it once was. In these circumstances many people will turn to pills of one sort or another which make them feel better *without giving up what they are doing* or waiting for nature or the crisis to take its course.

Sadly, many medical physicians find it expedient to dispense pills as a palliative measure against our ills. Fortunes are spent annually encouraging us to reach for this tranquilliser, or that sleeping pill.

For an increasing number of people drug-taking in one form or another has become a dominant part of life. Artificial substitutes help them stay awake, go to sleep or 'make it through life'. The net result is that feelings of self-control abate, there is a loss of self-confidence and 'pill-popping' becomes the central reinforcer in their lives. Once this pattern is entrenched, behaviour routines become organised around it. Problems are not faced and dealt with but are set aside and left unresolved. Even non-addicted people who lean on temporary psychological props during recovery from an emotional upheaval (a broken love affair or a divorce) often find it difficult to break the pill habit. Unless the instigating problem is coped with in other ways than with pills, a prolonged neurotic pattern will develop and ultimately become a way of life.

Neurosis—loss of joy in living

When someone feels persistently threatened by the potential dangers of life and unable to cope with them, he or she may gradually come to rely to a large extent on a neurotic defence pattern. These patterns are characterised by a loss of meaning and joy in life. The neurotic typically feels helpless and useless and acts so as to lessen discomfort or 'unpleasure' rather than attain positive accomplishment. A system of defences quickly becomes an ineffective way of coping with life, and will be regarded by psychologists as abnormal.

The loss of joy.

The most common of the neurotic responses is *anxiety neurosis*. Throughout the Western world, tens of millions of us suffer from anxiety neurosis. One in six readers of this book may well have consulted a general medical practitioner about the problem. 'Why do I experience so much anxiety? Where does it come from?' Medical examinations reveal no organic causes and the individual is pronounced perfectly healthy. But neurotics know and feel otherwise. Failing to cope with overwhelming anxiety, their minds 'pound away'. They have heart palpitations, perspiration and muscular pains; attacks of breathlessness continue to plague their bodies. A declaration of 'no known medical cause' simply feeds the cycle of anxiety which, in turn, entrenches feelings of helplessness.

Psychologists call this phenomenon 'free-floating anxiety', because it does not appear to be anchored to a specific source. Psychotherapy is used to try and identify the source of the problem and institute a reasonable way of handling it.

'I'm afraid of it'

Anxiety does not seem so irrational a response to urban surroundings as desolate as these.

People with *phobias* tack their 'free-floating anxiety' on to an object around them. However, the object is typically not a source of physical harm or danger. Phobics realise the irrationality of their reaction—but this realisation only serves to make their anxiety worse. There are many theories about phobias, but one way of explaining the phenomenon is that a phobic tries to handle serious internal conflicts by externalising them. If something is

'out there', the phobic can say: 'I'm afraid of it and it's best I never go near it'. But in reality it is the 'self' which is being avoided. Self-confrontation is usually too painful, so the external object epitomises all that should be avoided.

For most phobics the feared objects are not easily avoidable. In fact, the phobia changes the context of their lives completely. The prospect of going outside, or crossing the road, seeing a bird or a spider, may terrify them to the point of total incapacitation— which may be, of course, the true but unrecognised purpose of acquiring the phobia.

But behavioural psychologists have successfully treated a large number of phobics. For example, there are many for whom train travel poses a serious threat. Treatment for this fear would begin with a train journey in a group together with their therapist, and then without him but with the members of the group able to comfort one another along the way and work through their mutual anxieties. Finally, they would be made to travel individually. There is a certain risk that removing the symptom in this way may result only in some other symptom manifesting itself (you lose your fear of trains but become terrified of snow, say); but in general such symptomatic treatment seems to work because the symptom itself so powerfully symbolises the real trouble.

Obsessional behaviour

Another neurotic behaviour pattern is thought to stem from guilt feelings and repressed desires. This is the *obsessive-compulsive neurosis* which incorporates two separate reactions. They occur together so frequently that they are clinically regarded as being two aspects of a single behaviour pattern.

Most people have recurrent nagging thoughts: 'Did I leave the car lights on?' 'Did I lock the front door?' A popular tune sometimes 'sticks' stubbornly in one's head for hours. These niggling thoughts are trivial when compared to neurotic obsessional thoughts which disrupt life and can disable an individual completely. Such neurotics are unable to concentrate on anything but the obsessions which occupy their thoughts.

Obsessive thoughts appear to act as a buffer between the neurotic's feelings and actions. They constitute a new kind of 'reality'—something which must be dealt with. Compulsions facilitate the translation of these thoughts into behaviour, usually consisting of highly repetitive and ritualistic actions. One patient was known to have spent most of seven months climbing in and out of bed every morning. He stood up, crossed the floor, then forgot his initial movements. Back to bed he would go, reattempting the manoeuvre over and over again.

Preoccupation with intricate and complicated rituals is the obsessive-compulsive's means of ensuring that unconscious impulses being guarded against are shut out. Some rituals—such as the persistent necessity to 'cleanse oneself' by constant hand-washing—are even designed symbolically to undo guilt feelings.

Avoiding the unpleasant

When last did you 'just happen' to forget that dreaded dental appointment? Has it ever occurred to you to wonder why sick-leave during school examinations suddenly escalates?

We all tend to try and avoid unpleasant situations. But when this type of defence is taken to its extreme and includes an actual loss of motor or sensory function, psychologists describe it as *hysterical neurosis.*

Some years ago, a young couple had their first child. The husband was on his way to the hospital to see his baby for the first time when he was involved in an automobile smash. Although quite uninjured, he stumbled away totally blind. Intensive ophthalmic investigation revealed no organic reasons for his blindness. Four months later, a clinical psychologist solved the mystery.

The man had been opposed to having a child in the first year of marriage and was bitter about the fact that his wife had conceived under false pretences. Could he have purposely crashed the car, not wanting to get to the hospital? Did he go blind in order not to set eyes on his child—the source of his resentment? When he was offered this interpretation, the man's sight was miraculously restored.

This is an example of what is known as *conversion hysteria*—and it is not an isolated case. Incidents involving a sudden loss of speech, sight, hearing and feeling—all without medical foundation—are well documented. In each case hysterical symptoms were sustained as long as the underlying conflicts remained unresolved.

Another form of wiping out a system of failed 'coping processes' and an unhappy past is *amnesia.* The amnesiac 'disowns' himself to avoid unbearable internal conflict. He gives himself a blank cheque to start a new life.

An even more extreme case of disassociation is termed *multiple personality* (popularised in the film and book *The Faces of Eve*). Here two (sometimes more) distinct personalities are developed, each ruling the individual's life at different times. The currently dominating personality tends to contrast with the one in recession. It is not unusual to have 'good/bad' or 'extrovert/introvert' type personalities alternating. These seem to symbolise the subject's inner conflicts.

Hypochondria is yet another kind of neurotic response. Most people have been lightly accused (or have accused others) of being hypochondriacs. Clinical hypochondria, however, is a serious problem, and those who suffer it are really ill. Typically the hypochondriac has a morbid preoccupation with every minor bodily ailment, thinking that it is the first sign of a very serious disease. Some psychologists feel that hypochondriacs enjoy their 'poor health' as a means of gaining 'secondary attention' such as sympathy and service from others. Hypochondriacs also take great solace in finding 'terrible' symptoms which support their predictions about their pending doom. By doing so they satisfy themselves that they are 'physically ill' rather than mentally ill, since mental illness is unacceptable to most people—even hypochondriacs.

Mad with grief?

Depressive neurosis is characterised by distortion of reality; over-exaggeration of problems, 'seeing black everywhere' and being intensely sad about it all for an abnormally long period of time. Hand-in-glove with this morbid state go such complaints as irritability, boredom, lack of concentration, sleep and appetite, poor self-image and eventually poor physical health.

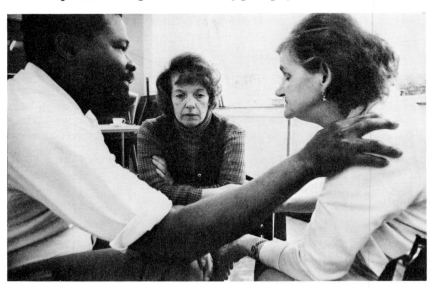

Depressive neurosis: the comforting hand may be no more help than being told to 'snap out of it'.

Neurotic depression usually emerges as the result of the loss of someone close, a failure of sorts, or even through constant frustration. There is little or no connection between the reality of what has happened and the individual's subjective evaluation of it. To the depressive, subjective reality is the *only* reality, and this is always tinged with fatalism, unhappiness and pain. It is quite common for depressives to take 'pick-me-up' drinks and drugs, just to keep going from day to day.

The ups and downs

In *manic-depressive* disorders fits of severe *depression* alternate with periods of *mania* (although in some cases only one of these conditions may manifest itself). It is not in most cases a continuous illness: about half those who have it suffer only a single attack, but others may experience repeated attacks over a period of a year or years.

The manic phase is characterised by lively behaviour, enthusiasm, increased alertness and sensory perceptions (the lights may look brighter, noises sound louder), much movement and great self-confidence. These symptoms may indeed sound very desirable, but the tolerable form can quite suddenly give way to *acute mania*, in which there may be confusion, delusions of omniscience and omnipotence, insensitivity to others, aggressiveness (especially in response to criticism), and hallucinations. This phase may perhaps be an attempt by the sufferer to stave off the depressive part of the cycle, getting worse as desperation sets in.

The alternate phase, *depression*, produces feelings of hopelessness and inability to take pleasure in anything—and these can grow progressively worse. Allied with sleeplessness—depressives characteristically sleep only four or five hours—and consequent fatigue, the sufferer may lose all power to act (but may, curiously, rally at about five o'clock every afternoon), and become obsessed with thoughts of sin and death. Suicide is a real risk, especially after the trough of depression has been passed and some energy returns. Before that it is possible to be too depressed to take suicidal action.

Many cases of manic depression are now thought to be due to biochemical imbalances, and it may even be partly hereditary. But it can also be associated with an overload of responsibility in childhood. It is often sucessfully treated with drugs, which may have to be taken as a prophylactic regime.

What is a psychotic?

The old joke has it that a neurotic knows that three and three make six—and worries about it . . . a psychotic knows that three and three make seven and is quite happy about it. But it is no laughing matter. Psychosis is far more deviant and pathologically intense than neurosis: psychotics lose touch with reality as they act out their fantasies in life; they are usually quite barren of emotion, and appear shabby and disorientated. Since they do not differentiate between their own (subjective) reality and the real (objective) world around them, they do not understand that their behaviour is unusual or bizarre. It follows that the social restraints and behavioural rules applying to 'normal' people are non-existent for psychotics. They act out prevailing thoughts and feelings without inhibition—and with no pangs of guilt, shame or anxiety.

A psychosis is not simply an extension of a neurotic illness—neurotics do not ordinarily become psychotics. The dividing line between the two is stark and dramatic.

There are two main categories of psychoses. If a psychotic reaction is caused by some physical ailment, such as brain damage or biochemical imbalance, it is called *organic psychosis*. *Functional psychoses*, on the other hand, have their roots in a breakdown of behavioural function somewhere along the line. The functional psychoses include three well-known psychotic states: *paranoid* reactions, *affective* reactions and *schizophrenic* reactions.

Delusions, delusions

Two psychotics were having a heated argument in their ward about which one of them was Moses. 'I know I'm Moses. God told me so!' said one with conviction. A third patient, who had been looking on, cut in: 'Not true, not true. I never told you anything of the sort.' No, still no laughing matter: these psychotics were suffering from delusions, which are characteristic of paranoid psychosis. In this instance it was *delusions of grandeur.*

Another type of delusion which is common in the paranoid state is that of *reference.* When this delusion takes hold, psychotics see everything that is happening around them as being aimed against them. For example, two old people sitting innocently on a park bench may appear to the tormented psychotic to be plotting his or her death. Delusions of persecution are similar to those of reference. 'Everyone dislikes me—they are all against me', complains the typical sufferer.

It is believed that those who have an overwhelming guilt about some kind of immoral behaviour are particularly prone to paranoiac persecution delusions. Other precipitators of paranoia are thought to be intense inferiority complexes and unrealistically high goals in life. Research has shown that paranoiacs generally come from higher socio-economic status levels than other maladjusted patients. They also tend to be intellectually superior.

The shattered perceptions of paranoia ...

Schizophrenia

About one person in 100, in any culture for which figures are known, will develop the disorder of schizophrenia. The present-day upsurge of interest in it can be ascribed partly to the writings of R. D. Laing, who claimed that the schizophrenic reaction was the only sane way of dealing with an insane world. It was the rest of us, with our adjustment to the craziness of life, who were mad.

Whatever the merits of Laing's theories, the description of the condition is not in dispute. The schizophrenic's way of thinking characteristically does not match up with the reality that the rest of us know. Disordered perceptions and emotions mean that he or she receives quite different messages from the environment—and responds in what appear to be quite inappropriate ways. Extreme withdrawal is a common feature of schizophrenia.

Schizophrenics themselves have vividly described the perception-thought disorder experience: 'It's like trying to get somewhere but inevitably setting off in the wrong direction—and being led along side paths by the myriad different associations that come to mind from every word or object,' said one.

Types of schizophrenia range from the simple, with less obvious symptoms and a gradual withdrawal from people, to the 'silliness', and giggling, regressed mannerisms of the *hebephrenic*. A *paranoid* schizophrenic usually has persecutory or grandiose delusions and hallucinations and is frequently aggressive and hostile. *Catatonic* schizophrenia is characterised either by the assumption of fixed postures—trances—for hours on end, or excessive—sometimes violent—activity and excitement.

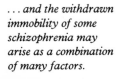

... and the withdrawn immobility of some schizophrenia may arise as a combination of many factors.

The origins of psychotic behaviour are still not clear to researchers, who are continuing their search for causes—and cures. Present-day researchers favour the view that many factors, genetic, biochemical, neurological and environmental, contribute to the cause of a psychotic illness such as schizophrenia.

9 Towards a better world

There is still to be found on bookstalls a publication which, in the heyday of the 'counter-cultures' was designed to provide those people looking for 'alternative' ways of living with some knowledge of everything they would need. It was called The Whole Earth Catalog. *Without in any way suggesting that psychology has the characteristics of a counter-culture or a counter-science, a book seeking to describe what psychology is could do worse than adapt that title for itself—A Whole Life Catalogue. Because the idea that psychology is something related only to specific areas of life—and sometimes unhealthy ones, at that—should long ago have been relegated to the corners of Man's museum where the Phlogiston Theory and Ptolemaic Astronomy moulder quietly away.*

No aspect of human life on this planet is, or need be, impervious to the attentions of psychology. Indeed, one could go farther and say that any aspect of animal life touched on by human beings will be amenable to psychological exploration and, eventually, explanation. This applies right down the line from we humans, complex and variable, to the simplest 'behaving' organisms, the amoebae, which are almost undifferentiated from one another and whose range of activity is severely limited. This huge scope, which has become apparent to psychologists and others only in recent decades, holds out great promise for coming to terms with kinds of problems that have never satisfactorily been dealt with before.

The ages of man

Just as this 'philosophy of the science of . . . life' (as B. F. Skinner has called it) covers the spectrum of behaving life, so it stretches its concern throughout the life of human beings, from the first stirring of the fetal senses to the last heartbeat on the deathbed—and even beyond: what we do with our dead is behaviour, too.

A life may be seen as a whole by the person living it, and to a lesser extent by those who love and know that person. But for those we do not know intimately, lives fall conveniently—and

We can be forgiven for
thinking that
'Chaos is come again'.

usefully for the purposes of study—into more or less distinct stages. Shakespeare's Jaques may first have told us about them, but they are equally convenient for psychologists. Among the primary divisions by which this discipline, like other scientific studies, informs itself are the developmental phases of life.

The Life Cycle series will in general follow this convenient distinction between ages and stages. There are volumes on pregnancy and birth, infancy, childhood, adolescence, family life, middle age, and ageing and death.

At one time childbirth was for doctors alone to see: now this scene seems more 'natural' and 'better for the children'. Is it a real advance or just the swing of the pendulum of fashion?

But the series will also address itself to matters which do not begin and end with the onset and growing out of developmental stages—matters which, as it were, run vertically through the horizontal divisions of age. *Anxiety* and stress can begin with fetal distress in a long labour and end only with the acceptance of death, all affairs put in order and the funeral paid for, at the end of the long labour of life. *Addictions* can begin before birth from a drug-taking mother and end with the last cigarette before the firing-squad. Neither *Sexuality* nor person-to-person relationships are confined to a single age of human life.

The world about us

At the beginning of this chapter the statement is made that 'no aspect of life ... need be ... impervious to the attentions of psychology'. It is one of the purposes of this book, and this series, to provide people with sufficient basic knowledge of the way they function—and *why* they function that way—to be able to understand the attention that the world we live in will, indeed *should*, increasingly demand from psychologists.

We live in a time of change which would seem wildly accelerated to even our recent ancestors. As has become evident in such extra 'visible' matters as high-rise housing and city architecture generally, too often change is under the direction and execution of those for whom 'people' exist only as an abstract. (If you think this is untrue or exaggerated, keep your ears open for the words used instead of 'people' by those with whom you come in contact in a professional or business relationship: 'workers'? 'clients'? 'patients'? 'caseload'? 'trade unionists'? 'management'? 'tenants'? 'human resources'? 'productive units'? 'operatives'? 'ratepayers'? You can make your own list: it will surprise you.)

Yet *people*, men, women and children, are the users, the buyers, the sufferers or the beneficiaries of change. It must be primarily to the way people are and behave and hope that change should conform, in any society which pretends to be interested in the welfare of its members. We have all seen 'architectural' pedestrian precincts and playgrounds which *look* interesting or even beautiful, but in which no man, woman or child will ever walk or play with pleasure. We have all, too, come up against a bureaucracy in which what causes its members the least trouble is the first consideration, and the solution of our problems the last.

It has been truly said that 'it is much less expensive . . . to hire a thousand psychologists than to make even a miniscule change in the social . . . structure'.[1] But the influence of psychology need not be merely cosmetic. There *are* open spaces in which people enjoy themselves because their planner has taken the trouble to find out what people do and how they do it. There *are* classrooms in which learning is efficient and teacher–pupil relations are good because trouble has been taken to apply the principles—of learning theory and personal relationships—psychology has uncovered. There have been wars averted, crises resolved, because the potential antagonists never lost sight of each other's humanity and understood each other's attitudes and motives. And there are families for whom only a little insight into what makes children, adolescents, parents behave as they do has meant the difference between disastrous conflict and reasonable harmony.

The way ahead

To claim that psychology can cure all the ills of the world would be ridiculous. Yet a list of the problems that are inevitably going to be of most concern to our world will produce a significant number that can perhaps be influenced by a thorough knowledge of how people behave.

Overpopulation is our nightmare. Would compulsory sterilisation or euthanasia alleviate it? If it would, what would the collective psychological impact be on those affected by it and in turn, what kind of society would result? Could people, instead, be induced, conditioned, to breed less damagingly? In case of disaster, could the process be reversed? Could the obvious disaster—nuclear war—be averted?

These are not political problems. Only the actions taken are the business of politics. If we are aware enough of the knowledge and the techniques which psychology has made available, we can make sure, at least, that our interests as people are taken account of in those political actions. At present, that knowledge and those techniques are too thinly spread among *us*, but well taken up by *them*—governments, commissions, commerce, armies. The fact that we use the words 'us' and 'them' means that where there should be interaction, there is none.

Uncommon sense

Where psychologists are asked to intervene in matters that would at one time have been left to 'common sense', it sometimes seems that what was common was not all that sensible. What would you do, as a western American sheepfarmer, if coyotes were preying on your flocks? The answer the farmers gave was: 'Shoot the coyotes.' But conservation in today's world extends even to coyotes, and a better solution came from the psychologists. Aversion conditioning is a technique used to break addictions or to reform undesirable behaviour in human beings, notably those hooked on alcohol. Taken from the psychotherapist's clinic to the sheeplands, it proved just as effective on coyotes. Baits of sheepmeat dosed with an emetic drug switched them from sheep to an alternative—rabbits.

Obviously there are matters a lot nearer home that will bear a close look from psychology. Are women the 'weaker sex'? Recent investigations seem to indicate that women have better physiological control than men have. There is much more—from the relatively trivial (why do people like to frighten themselves at horror movies or on fairground rides?) to the fundamentally important (why does a four-year-old learn, say, Chinese faster and better than a university student by all other indicators at the height of his learning potential?).

Were it not for the direction in which the observation of people's behaviour has gone—from classification by 'humours' to controlled psychological experimentation—there would now be no way for us to tackle such problems of what we are and how we behave, no reliable or consistent starting-point from which to begin the slow, hard business of understanding ourselves.

That is what the *Life Cycle* series is all about.

References

2   The soft machine

1. Burroughs, W. *The Soft Machine*. London: Calder, 1968.
2. Holden, C. 'Psychosurgery: Legitimate Therapy or Laundered Lobotomy?'. *Science*, 1973, 179, 1109–1112.
3. Kellog, W. N. 'Sonar System of the Blind'. *Science*, 1962, 137, 399–404.
4. Hebb, D. O. 'Drives and the C.N.S.'. *Psychological Review*, 1955, 62, 243.

3   We live and learn

1. Pavlov, I. P. *Conditioned Reflexes*. (Trans. by G. V. Anrep.) NY: Oxford, 1927.
2. Watson, J. B. *Psychology from the Standpoint of a Behaviourist*. Philadelphia, Pa.: Lippincott, 1924.
3. Skinner, B. F. *Science and Human Behaviour*. NY: Macmillan, 1948.
4. Verhave, T. The pigeon as a quality-control inspector. In R. Ulrich, T. Stachnik, and J. Mabry (Eds.), *Control of Human Behaviour*. Glenview, Ill.: Scott, Foresman, 1966. .
5. Padelino, E. Reported in *Psychology Today* (British edition) May 1975. 1, 2, 10–11.
6. Azrin, N. H. & Foxx, R. M. *Toilet Training the Retarded*: a rapid program for day and night time independent toileting. Champaign, Ill.: Research Press, 1973.
7. Harlow, H. F. The Foundation of Learning Sets. *Psychological Review*, 1949, 56, 51–65.
8. Rosenfeld, H. M. 'Conversational Control Functions of Nonverbal Behaviour'. In A. W. Siegman and S. Feldstein (Eds.), *Nonverbal Behaviour and Communication*. Hillsdale, New Jersey: Erlbaum, 1978.
9. Breland, K. & Breland, M. The misbehaviour of organisms. *American Psychologist*, 1961, 16, 681–684.
10. Zimbardo, P. G. & Ruch, F. L. *Psychology and Life*. Ninth Ed. Glenview, Ill.: Scott, Foresman and Co., 1975.
11. Miller, N. E. *Selected Papers*. Chicago: Aldine Atherton, 1971.

4   Remembering and forgetting

1. Luria, A. *The Mind of a Mnemonist*. NY: Avon Books, 1969.
2. Lashley, K. S. *The Neuropsychology of Lashley*: selected papers. NY: McGraw-Hill, 1960, 478–505.
3. Tulving, E. *Remembering and forgetting*. Paper presented at the British Psychological Society's annual conference. University of York, 1978.

5   Looking for a motive

1. Davis, C. M. Self-selection of diet by newly weaned infants. *American Journal of Diseases of Children*, 1928, 36, 651–679.
2. Nisbett, R. E. & Schachter, S. The cognitive manipulation of pain. *Journal of Experimental Social Psychology*, 1966, 2, 227–236.
3. Maslow, A. H. *Motivation and personality*. NY: Harper & Row, 1954.

4. Taylor, F. W. *Scientific Management.* NY: Harper & Row, 1947.
5. Mayo, E. *The Social Problems of an Industrial Civilization.*
   London: Routledge & Kegan Paul, 1975.
6. Herzberg, F. *Work and the Nature of Man.* World Publishing Co.,
   1966.
7. McClelland, D. C. *The Achieving Society.*
   Englewood Cliffs, N. J.: Prentice-Hall, 1968.
8. Winter, D. G. 'Picking a President—what makes the
   candidates run'. *Psychology Today,* July 1976, 10, 2, 45–49.

6 Revealing our feelings

1. Schachter, S. & Singer, J. Cognitive, social, and physiological
   determinants of emotional state. *Psychological Review,*
   1962, 69, 379–399.
2. Beecher, H. K. Generalization from pain of various type
   and diverse origins. *Science,* 1959, 130, 267–268.
3. Delgado, J. M. R. *Physical Control of the Mind:*
   Toward a Psychocivilized Society. NY: Harper & Row, 1969.
4. Bandura, A. Influence of models' reinforcement contingencies
   on the acquisition of imitative responses.
   Journal of Personality and Social Psychology, 1965, 1, 589–595.
5. Bandura, A., Ross, D., & Ross, S. A.
   Imitation of film-mediated aggressive models.
   Journal of Abnormal and Social Psychology, 1963, 66, 3–11.

7 'I am that I am'

1. Westman, J. C. *Individual Differences in Children.*
   NY: Wiley—Interscience, 1973.
2. Hartshorne, H., & May, M. A. Studies in the Nature of Character.
   Vol. 1. *Studies in deceit.* NY: Macmillan, 1928.
3. Williams, R. J. *Biochemical individuality.* NY: Wiley, 1956.
4. Jung, C. G. The Collected Works. Vol. 6. *'Psychological Types'.*
   London: Routledge & Kegan Paul, 1971.
5. Rogers, C. R. *On Becoming a Person:* A therapist's view
   of psychotherapy. Boston: Houghton Mifflin, 1961.
6. Freud, S. *Three Essays on the Theory of Sexuality.*
   London: The Hogarth Press & The Institute of
   Psychoanalysis, 1905.
7. Erikson, E. *Childhood and Society.* NY: W. W. Norton and Co, Inc., 1963.

8 Going off the rails

1. Benedict, R. Rituals. In *The Encyclopedia of Social Sciences.*
   NY: Macmillan, 1935.
2. Laing, R. D. *The Divided Self.* London: Tavistock Publications.
   Penguin Books, 1959.
3. Szasz, T. *The Age of Madness.* Garden City, NY: Anchor Press, 1973.
4. Rosenhan, D. L. On being sane in insane places. *Science,* 1973,
   179, 250–258.

9 Towards a better world

1. Bazelon, D. L. Cited in Caplan, N., & Nelson, S. On being useful.
   American Psychologist, 1973, 28(3), 199–211.

Suggested further reading

Evans, P. *Motivation.* London: Methuen, 1975.
Evans, R. I. *The Making of Psychology: discussions with creative contributors.*
    NY: Alfred A. Knopf, Inc., 1976.
Gregory R. L. *The Intelligent Eye.* NY: McGraw-Hill, 1970.
Hebb, D. O. What psychology is about. *American Psychologist,*
    1974, 29, 71–79.
Kaplan, B. (Ed.) *The Inner World of Mental Illness.* NY:
    Harper & Row, 1964.
Skinner, B. F. *About Behaviourism.* NY: Vintage Books—Random House, 1974.
Smith, R. E., Sarason, I. G., & Sarason, B. R., *Psychology:*
    The frontiers of behaviour. NY: Harper & Row Publishers, 1978.
Toffler, A. *Future Shock.* NY: Random House, 1970.

Index

126

Photo credits

A. K. P. Studios–81, 92; G. Alon (Monitin)–116; Applied Psychology Unit (MRC) Cambridge–6; Maria Bartha–91; Herbert Bishko–13; Yael Braun–15; By courtesy of British Airways–17 (*bottom*); Camera Press–38, 46 (*bottom*), 87; Ron Chapman–39, 40, 75, 79, 86; John Cohen–63; Colorific–5; Cusack–8; Gadi Dagon–24; Electricity Council–23; Avi Ganor–12; Henry Grant–21, 29, 52, 117; Greenhill–120; Tony Grylla (Rex)–99; Ferdinand Hodler–110; IBM Corporation–26; Ikon–90, 106; Israel Sun–84 (*top*); Robert Judges–111; Judy Kristal–95; B. A. Lewis–28; David McEnery (Rex)–46 (*top*), 61, 74 (*top*), 76; Lisa Mackson–4, 14, 16, 17 (*top*), 19, 25, 64, 66, 68 (*top*), 69, 73, 93; Mansell Collection–108; Leonard Nader (Globe Photos; Rex)–54; National Film Archive/Still Library–47; Moshe Orbach–65; Judy & Kenny Lester–89, 105; Palantetaan (Rex)–102; President's Selection Ltd., St. Peter's Road, Huntingdon, Cambridgeshire–85; Rex Features–7, 11, 22, 32, 35 (*top right*), 36, 37, 51, 55, 68 (*bottom*), 80, 119; Christopher Schwartz–109; Barry Sheridan–114; Sipa Press (Rex)–84 (*bottom*); 'Stern/Pix Features'–96; Homer Sykes–67, 82, 98, 101; Syndication International–74 (*bottom*), 78; Robert Taylor (Rex)–59; John Walmsley–45; Valerie Wilmer–44; Zefa–77.